THE STEP CHILD

THE
STEP
CHILD

A true story of a broken childhood

Donna Ford

Vermilion
LONDON

1 3 5 7 9 10 8 6 4 2

Published in 2007 by Vermilion, an imprint of Ebury Publishing

First published in 2006 in hardback by Vermilion

A Random House Group Company

The Random House Group Limited Reg. No. 954009

Addresses for companies within the Random House Group can be found at:
www.randomhouse.co.uk

A CIP cataogue record for this book is available from the British Library

The Random House Group Limited makes every effort to ensure that the
papers used in our books are made from trees that have been legally
sourced from well-managed and credibly certified forests. Our paper
procurement policy can be found on www.randomhouse.co.uk

Mixed Sources
Product group from well-managed
forests and other controlled sources
www.fsc.org Cert no. TT-COC-2139
© 1996 Forest Stewardship Council

To buy books by your favourite authors and register for offers visit
www.rbooks.co.uk

Typeset by SX Composing DTP, Rayleigh, Essex
Printed and bound in Great Britain by
CPI Cox and Wyman, Reading, RG1 8EX

ISBN 9780091910495

⤳

CONTENTS

༄

INTRODUCTION

WHEN I STARTED THIS BOOK, I didn't know exactly what I wanted. But I knew I wanted to tell my story.

As a little girl I had no voice. No one ever listened to my cries for help. I eventually stopped asking for forgiveness. I stopped asking for reassurance. I stopped asking for food. I stopped asking to go to the toilet. I stopped asking if I could get dressed to keep warm. Words didn't bring help or comfort – they brought only anger and hatred. Just as I stopped asking for things, I also stopped hoping. The social services turned a blind eye to my life. The school seemed blinkered to bruises, and bones sticking out from starvation. I was not just a child without a voice – I was the invisible girl too.

My life is different now. I have three children whom I have reared with love and respect. I have tried to instil in them a good sense of who they are. They are always listened to and their opinions are valued; they do not live with fear or guilt. In spite of the abuse I suffered as a child I have gone on to achieve my personal goals of being a good parent and nurturing my artistic talent, allowing me to earn a living from something I truly love to do. I can enjoy healthy, balanced relationships based on trust.

I am lucky because I am happy. This is my vindication.

My reasons for writing this book and telling my story are numerous, but my main one is to give that child – that me from that time – her voice. Although my story is horrific, I hope it will bring some encouragement that we can survive child abuse, and move on to become caring, thriving, balanced adults – not because of what is done to us, but despite it. It is a terrible way to learn to be a good parent, but for too long society has denied not only what happens to victims of abuse but also what becomes of those children when they grow up.

I don't know what you will make of my story, or indeed if you will care. But I hope it makes you think about your role as an adult in the life of any child whose path you cross. Every child has a right to be loved, nurtured, respected and educated. Not abused, not beaten, not starved, not used as an object. The child abuse statistics haven't changed much since I was a child. I am one of those statistics. I've waited 30 years for justice and to tell my story, and here it is. Now I can close those chapters of my life and move forward.

Donna Ford, November 2005

This is the story of a little girl . . . and a wicked stepmother.

Like all stories which start that way, the little girl was good – but was always told she was evil; while the stepmother had more badness in her than anyone could imagine.

But the little girl could imagine. She knew exactly how malevolent the stepmother was. She was the one who lived a life so terrible that the grown-ups couldn't even bring themselves to open their eyes to what was going on.

This book is about what happened to that little girl and that wicked stepmother.

It is for the woman that little girl became – a woman I now call a friend.

It is for the daughter of that woman – who was told reworked stories of Snow White with her mother at the centre of them.

It is for all the other little girls and boys out there who are still living lives like this. And whose stories we are still not listening to.

Linda Watson-Brown
November 2005

ぅ

PROLOGUE

Edinburgh, 1967

My name is Donna Ford.
I am eight years old.
And I am a really, really, really bad little girl.

I'M BAD AND I'M ugly and I deserve all the things that happen to
me. I'm an evil little witch. I can't remember any of the bad things
I do; I can't remember any of the evil that I spread; but I know it
must be true because my stepmother keeps telling me. She tells
me every time she slaps me. She tells me every time she punches
my stomach. She tells me every time she kicks me when I'm lying
on the floor.

I'm standing here today and I've been bad again. Maybe I said
a bad word. Once I said 'bloody' and then I had to get beaten.
Maybe I looked at my stepmother in an evil way. Sometimes I
look like she thinks my real Mummy must have looked and then
I have to be punished. It's hard to tell what I've done this time,
but there must have been something. I must have done something
to deserve it. And that will be why I'm standing here. In our
bathroom. In my vest and pants.

It's so cold. I've been here since this morning, and although I don't have a watch or a clock to tell the time, I know that it's been a while because it's getting dark now. I know that the others – my stepmother, my stepbrothers – have had a morning snack and some lunch and something else to eat after that, and now I can hear them getting dinner ready. I won't get out to eat dinner – and I wouldn't have had anything for lunch either. I don't get much to eat because I'm so bad. Maybe if I get out when they've all gone to bed, I can sneak into the larder and get a handful of cornflakes. That would be bad though – and I'd get punished if I get caught.

The cold is biting into me now. I hate this room, hate this bathroom. I spend so much time here, days like this, one after the other. When I do something bad, something she doesn't like, she screams at me and sends me here. I have to take off all my clothes, but if I'm lucky I get to keep my vest and knickers on.

I have to stand completely still. Sometimes in the bath, some-times on the floor. Sometimes facing the window, sometimes facing the wall. She says that she will know if I move at all, even if I move an inch. And she would know that – she knows everything. The weird feeling starts in my legs. My toes get very, very cold, so cold that I can't really feel them. Then, even weirder, the cold doesn't start shooting through my legs straight away. That's what you'd expect, isn't it? You'd think that the cold would spread up and up and up, but it seems to take a break. It gets my toes all frozen up, then stops, then starts on my fingers. It's only once all my toes and fingers are icy that the rest of me starts to feel it. My nose. My cheeks. My legs. My arms. The space on my tummy where my too-short vest doesn't meet my too-small knickers. I get all goose-bumpy, and then even the goose-bumps are too cold to stay.

I've tried lots of ways of not feeling so bad when she sends me in here. I just wish I could find something that works. Sometimes I try to think of nothing, to just make my mind go completely blank. Other times, I make up lists in my head, or invent a world from a book I've read, or use my eyes to trace patterns in the cracks in the wall. One day, I tried to listen to absolutely everything that was going on in the rest of the house. I could hear them all talking and laughing and just getting on with things. I could hear normal family stuff going on – meals being made, the kettle boiling, the radio being switched on and off. But that wasn't a good day. It dragged on forever. Every little thing I heard seemed to sound louder and last longer than it would if I wasn't standing here in this freezing cold room. I just have to wait on the seconds and minutes and hours passing, and then hope I'll be told to go back to my room without making her even more angry at me.

Today, I've got a problem. Before I was sent in here, I had a glass of water. Now I need the toilet. But I can't use the one that stands in front of me. I'm not allowed. If I use that, I will have to move. And I'm not allowed to move. If I ask to go to the loo, I'll have to talk. And I'm not allowed to talk. I can't even use the toilet when other people come in. That happens a lot – my stepbrother comes in and pees in front of me, and I have to stand there in silence, not moving, listening to the rush of his piss in the toilet and desperately wanting to do that myself. He calls me names and tries to provoke me because he knows that if I answer back, or nip him, then it's me who will get into trouble. So I have to stand there like a statue, and take whatever he throws at me.

I can't stop thinking about going to the loo. I've been standing here for hours, and I've got even more hours to go, but I can't do the most natural thing in the world, the thing that everyone else does in this room. This has happened before, and I've got to work out what would be for the best. If I do ask to go I'll get battered. If I don't ask I'll have to piss myself – and I'll probably get battered for that too. If I do just let it go, then at least I'll get a bit of heat while it runs down my leg. That doesn't last though, and it'll go cold really quickly and there'll be a smell. Tomorrow's a school day, and she won't let me get washed before then. I know I'll have to wet myself – I don't really have a choice – and I'll have to do it a few times if I'm in here as long as usual. It's the smell I hate when I go to bed and have to lie in my wet knickers, and then I get up in the morning and I've been lying in it all night, and when I go to school the other kids call me names and refuse to sit next to me because I stink.

My tummy hurts. It hurts from needing the loo, and it hurts from being punched most days, and it hurts so much from being hungry all the time.

My head hurts too. I get headaches because I go from being in the dark most of the time to bright light when I'm dragged out of my room. It aches from thinking about what I need to do, how to avoid my stepmother and her anger, how to behave from one day to the next, whether to cry and risk her getting really cross at me again, whether to shut myself off and risk it even more.

My body hurts from being kicked and hit practically every day. I may be small and skinny, but it doesn't stop my stepmother using me as a punchbag. I'm never without bruises. The fact that most other kids have bruises too doesn't help; it makes me feel worse to know that they get theirs from playing, from climbing trees and mucking about. I'm not really allowed out to play or to have friends. My bruises come from other things. My back aches and I'm sore all over. There's barely a place on me that she hasn't battered.

But most of all, my heart hurts.

I don't want this to keep happening.

I don't want to be a bad girl any longer.

I don't want to be without a real mummy.

I want this hell to stop.

Edinburgh, 2003

The hell never did stop.

I'm 44 years old. I'm married with three wonderful children. I'm a successful artist with a history of acclaimed exhibitions and commissions. And I'm sitting in Edinburgh's High Court looking at a woman I haven't seen for 30 years.

Helen Ford is standing in the dock. She looks much smaller than she did the last time we had anything to do with each other.

Back when she was my stepmother.

Back when she locked me in cupboards.

Back when she starved me, beat me, tortured me.

Back when she organised her parties, turned the music up louder, and laughed while the men she called her friends raped and abused me in our home.

When I left this morning, my six-year-old daughter asked me what I was going to do. I told her that when I was little, a woman called Helen had been mean to me, but now, today, someone in charge would be telling her she had to say sorry. My daughter takes it all in, trusts every simplified word. Whether I believe it myself is another matter. The hope that someone might finally listen is more than I can dare to believe.

I didn't ask for this.

I haven't brought this case.

I haven't sought retribution, or revenge, or even justice for what she did to me all those years ago.

I have pushed all this from my mind for so long that my head and body are in shock from having to face these memories.

This woman standing in front of me looks so innocuous. She is completely unmemorable to people she passes every day of her life. She could be any woman in her late 50s going through a perfectly normal day. Her hair is short, plain, unstyled. Her face is free from make-up. Her dark jacket and tapered trousers are unexceptional. Her white blouse and court shoes anonymous.

She still wears big prescription glasses as she did when I was little. But Helen Ford looks like an unremarkable woman.

Over five days, she won't flinch when asked about battering me when I was little more than a toddler. She will not weaken when it is put to her that she regularly smashed my face into the mirror, fed me dog food, made me stand almost naked for hours in a bath, forced me to clean the house with a nailbrush, threatened to flail me within an inch of my life. She will not baulk when asked for any justification, any reasoning for imprisoning a child and refusing to feed it. The questions will not upset her. Why was I malnourished? Why did I steal food from the pockets of classmates at school? Helen Ford answers in monosyllables whenever she can. She shows no emotion at any stage of the proceedings.

She stands there accused of 'procuring a child for sexual abuse' and it barely registers on her face. But I am that child. It was me who was procured. It was me who shivered in terror every time I heard the music outside my room get louder and the handle on my door turn. It was me who knew the fear of being sent on 'errands' to local men who would abuse me as easily as they would say 'hello' to their neighbours. It was me who lay on my bed petrified, awaiting the ring of the doorbell which signalled another of Helen's 'friends' had come to rape her eight-year-old stepdaughter.

And I'm waiting. I'm waiting for the story to end, for some reason, some explanation to appear and make sense of the memories I have denied for so long.

I'm waiting for her to say 'sorry' . . .

Chapter One

> ৵

BREDA'S BABIES

I HAD A MUMMY once. But I lost her.

Her name was Breda. Was. Is. I'm not sure – she may be reading this now; she may be dead. In my memory, my Mum can't be pinned down. Some records will say her name is Brenda; others that she was called Bridie. My Gran said once that it was Breda, and that seems to fit, so Breda she is.

I have a photograph of her on her wedding day. She is in white. There are four people in the picture. On the far left is Adam, the man who would be her first husband, the father of my elder half-brother. He is wearing a dark suit, his right leg slightly bent – it looks as if he is trying to make himself smaller to accommodate the tiny Breda standing next to him. My mother is dark-haired; she wears a short veil and a dress that ends some inches above her ankles. She carries a handbag and wears a corsage. A couple stands beside Breda and Adam – I have no idea who they are, or who they were to Breda at that time. Witnesses? Good friends who disappeared? Strangers dragged in off the street for the day?

No one in this picture looks particularly happy. They are standing on some paving slabs with a railing beside them and tall buildings either side. This area now has a shopping mall nearby, the St James Centre, one of the ugliest constructions in Edinburgh. It's hardly a scene of bridal delight. There is no joy in the photograph, nothing I can really hold on to. God knows I've tried. This is all I have of my mother. She looks so young, her dress too big for her, a girl playing at being a bride. And yet by the time this image was taken, she had already been the subject of scandal, ripped her own family apart, shamed them. Or so the legend goes. My own experience tells me that there will be another version of her life, another layer, as yet unheard – Breda's tale.

My mother was born and raised in County Tipperary in the Republic of Ireland. Her life began on 3 May 1935 but the details I have of her are few. What is known about Tipperary is that, like the rest of Ireland in the first half of the 20th century, times were hard for women. Most people will only have heard of the area through the song, 'It's a Long Way to Tipperary' – but outsider knowledge of the county itself is, like much of Ireland, more myth than dreary reality.

Any quick glance at a tourist brochure will give you the official angle – Tipperary is Ireland's largest inland county, completely landlocked. Those who have visited speak of its beauty, and the 2,300-feet-high Slievenamon mountain. That Slievenamon translates as 'mountain of the fairy woman' in Irish Gaelic is unsurprising – the Irish like their fairy tales as much as they like their theoretical admiration of women.

It's only real life that spoils things.

Breda Curran, my Mum, had three brothers that I know of – Pat, John and her eldest brother, Michael. In 1953, when she was only 18, she left Ireland along with Michael and headed for England. The details I have are sketchy, but I have been told that both my mother and Uncle Michael managed to find work in London, where they settled for a while. As time went on, things must have looked a lot better than Tipperary, as my maternal grandparents and their two other sons also came to these shores.

However, this was not a happy family set-up. Breda was considered headstrong – she was described as knowing her own mind; having a clear idea of what she wanted; not being backward at coming forward. To me, these phrases sound all too familiar, ways of simply putting down a young woman who was probably trying to get away from the shackles of an oppressive family life. Being an only girl in a family of boys, with staunch Catholic parents who themselves were living in a strange land, did not necessarily make Breda wild. It's an age-old story – a girl trying to break free of the straitjacket of stereotyping is always perceived to be so much more trouble than a boy doing the same thing.

Who knows whether Breda was truly a flighty soul, or whether she just decided to live up to the stories which were circulating about her anyway? Whatever the reason, she found herself in a relationship with a man who was not only considerably older, but also married, and a family member – her cousin.

It doesn't take psychic powers to work out where Breda was heading. The relationship with Robert Cummings was doomed, due to a lethal combination of his marital status and the disapproval of her family. This same family did not take kindly to their daughter's pregnancy at the age of 19. Hypocrisy is an emotion of enormous strength. The fact that girls had been messing about with boys and ending up with large bellies and shattered reputations since time immemorial did not stop the family from treating Breda as if she were the first ever to find herself in such a position.

Only recently has Ireland managed to shake off its reputation as the most sexually repressed country in Europe, where women were second-class citizens and the Catholic Church ruled virtually unchallenged. When Breda Curran was a young woman, the view that sex outside marriage was wrong permeated the society in which she lived – despite the fact that her family actually lived across the water. The Currans had brought their values with them – and Breda would pay the price.

The child of my mother and Robert Cummings would be my elder half-sister Frances. What happened between the pregnancy being announced, the relationship ending and Frances's early years has never been explained to me – it all became wrapped up in the package that was my mother's 'bad ways'. What is obvious is that the society in which the Currans lived had given them a set of principles which worked only in theory – and rarely for women. Sex for them was permitted only in marriage, and only really supported as part of the ultimate goal of having children. Enjoyment and freedom never came into the picture. Rarely did men feel the same restrictions.

I don't know whether my mother considered abortion as an option – if she had, there would have been ways and means of accessing an end to her first pregnancy – but for some reason she decided that her child would be born, despite the environment of disapproval and badmouthing it would inhabit. With all of this baggage, it's hard to see how Breda could have escaped the destiny hurtling towards her. Before long, she had a child out of wedlock by a married man. How or why she then ended up with Adam Robertson, the groom from the photograph I have, is a mystery to me. For not only did that marriage quickly turn sour, but Adam was also the nephew of Robert Cummings. Having moved to Edinburgh, the two were married on 7 August 1956. In October 1957, their son, Simon, was born. I now had a half-sister and a half-brother waiting for me.

Adam left, leaving Breda with both Frances and Simon. The family picture was becoming increasingly complicated. Due to the familial relationship between Robert and Adam, their two children with Breda were not only half-siblings, but also second cousins. My mother didn't take long to find someone else.

No one has ever really told me anything that I can hold on to as 'fact' about my conception. The only thing I know for sure is that my mother met Don Ford at a party. From all accounts, she 'took up' with him immediately. Is that because she found it so hard to imagine herself without a man? Was she actively looking for someone to step in and help her look after her two small children? Did she set out to get someone without any emotional attachment? Or is there a chance, just a chance, that my mother and father actually fell head over heels at that party? Perhaps it was passion at first sight; perhaps he was the one she felt a connection with; and perhaps I was conceived out of love.

I can cling to this latter story if I want to, because Breda wasn't as badly off as you might expect a single mother to be at that time. There seemed to have still been some sort of affection between her and Robert Cummings, the father of her first daughter, because it is alleged that he actually bought her the flat she was living in, at 31 Easter Road, Edinburgh. There is no doubt that he was financially comfortably off. I have been able to piece together parts of a story which suggest he bought the property both as a means of helping the mother of his child, and as an investment to leave to the daughter he could never fully recognise due to his other family.

The arrival of Don Ford on the scene did nothing to placate the Currans. Their daughter was an embarrassment to them – two children to two different men, and another soon on the way. There was some contact between the two families, but by the time I was born in June 1959, the damage was irreparable.

I have very few memories of our time as a family. They have been formed from what others have told me and, I suppose, what I would expect families to be like. My half-brother has told me that he remembers a day when we were all in the garden together and our mother was making daisy chains. I was sitting up in one of those old-fashioned coach-built prams, and he tells me that the scene was a happy one, that Breda was a warm, laughing woman. I can picture it – but I don't really remember it. Like many things, images such as this one have turned into what I want them to be, rather than what they were.

Happy family situations were not the norm, however. Simon

also remembers another time, with me still in the pram, and the air loud with shouting. My father was yelling and screaming at my mother, eventually slapping and pushing her. My brother was hanging on to her leg, and both of them fell against the side of my pram as Don Ford's temper got the better of him.

So, what is the truth? Were we a happy family, with a pretty, laughing mother making daisy chains? Or did we all live in fear of the latest man on the list, the one who happened to be my Dad, the one whose temper and anger laid the foundations of violence to come? Surely, like most families, there would be a combination of good and bad – but I can't remember. I have no memories of my mother at all. I know only the few snippets that others have told me, most of which are unreliable. I don't know when exactly, but I recall my Auntie Madge (my father's younger sister) telling me a bit about Breda – how she'd abandoned us, how I had pneumonia and malnutrition and was taken into care. On another occasion she changed her story to declare that we had all run away from our terrible Mum (conveniently forgetting that I was just a baby at the time), and it was only through the incredibly lucky coincidence of a group of friendly nuns finding us that we survived! It was all doom and gloom. Auntie Madge spoke in hushed tones so I worked out that the subject of my mother was not to be raised. Breda was a taboo subject. I do know from letters that there was little warmth between her and her own parents, and this extended to us. My maternal grandmother made it clear that she was only interested in Frances, the daughter of Robert Cummings, and wanted nothing to do with the rest of us.

Whatever the truth, the cards were marked for my parents.

Breda left Don.

She left Edinburgh.

She left her babies.

My mother was a product of her times. My half-siblings and I may have been growing up at the beginning of the 1960s, when women were told their worlds were changing, but for many of them, change was just a word. The sexual freedom and liberation which would come to characterise the period meant little to the girls and women who were still defined in terms of how their communities and families judged them.

I don't know why Breda finally disappeared. I only know the consequences of her actions.

Don Ford was left alone with three little children in an Edinburgh flat bought by another man. I would soon leave that flat – that inconsequential address – but I would never forget it. I would return to 31 Easter Road, and the next time I lived there, there would not even be the possibility of a happy memory. The daisy chain days were gone. And the nightmare for the little girl in the coach-built pram was only just beginning.

Chapter Two

༈

THIS LITTLE FAMILY

January 1961–July 1964

HALDANE HOUSE IS THE first home I can remember. The irony is that it was a Barnardo's children's residence, not some warm family two-up-two-down. In January 1961, I became one of Haldane House's 'inmates', and I remained there for three-and-a-half years. My mother had left us in October 1960, and for a few months my father had tried to look after me, his only biological child, and the two others he had found himself landed with. Myself, Simon and Frances were all still so young: Frances was five when Breda left, Simon three, while I had just turned one.

I have pieced together what happened to the three of us once our mother left from files, letters and documents. Throughout the pages of notes accumulated by Barnardo's, what strikes me are the condemnations of Breda. Under the heading 'Parents' Religion' are clear black capitals stating that my mother was a *lapsed* Roman Catholic. Another section outlines the fathers of each of her three children – alongside my name only is one word suffused with judgement and assumption: *putative*. The words continue – Breda *bore a very bad character* and *associated with many men*. Frances was her *first illegitimate child* and there were *subsequent disquieting reports* of my mother's conduct.

In black and white, the story of my mother's life and of our early years feels paltry. Everything is either sanitised or disapproving. Among these comments come fragments which do help to build the picture for me, but I can only guess at the full narrative.

It takes just one page of typed notes to cover our lives. My mother's early years in Edinburgh are glossed over quickly and disparagingly. 'Before her marriage, the mother gave birth to her first illegitimate child by a man ... who is uncle to her husband. Subsequently the mother was married ... in August 1956 and gave birth to one child in 1957.' This I know – these are the beginnings of Frances and Simon. But then I read something new. 'At about this time, the case became known to the RSSPCC [Royal Scottish Society for the Prevention of Cruelty to Children] for the mother bore a very bad character. The mother's husband worked and lived in Stirling, but his employer, a farmer, refused to have the mother near the place.' These are 'facts' I have no knowledge of. The involvement of the RSSPCC was a significant matter. The organisation was often referred to as 'the cruelty', and in the days before ChildLine, threats of 'I'll be getting the cruelty in' could often be heard. So, who had 'reported' my mother to 'the cruelty'? What, if anything, had she done? Was there physical abuse? Neglect? Were my siblings dirty or ill-clothed, hungry or beaten? Had neighbours heard something to make them concerned? Or had the Stirling farmer, who for some reason wouldn't let my mother near her husband's workplace, initiated RSSPCC involvement?

The report continues: 'The mother's husband had to be warned to provide for the mother, but he would maintain only his own child. Over the next few years, the mother moved to many addresses and was suspected of associating with many men. While at a party, three years ago, she met a man called Donald Ford, with whom she later cohabited, hoping to be married to him when she could obtain a divorce.' My mother's character was being blackened even further with each sentence –

described as moving on from man to man, from one relationship to another, she was now picking men up at parties and 'cohabiting'.

I don't know why she finally left my father. According to the Barnardo's reports, after settling in the basement flat at 31 Easter Road, and having me, there was an incident which may have precipitated the split. At one point, 'Ford, with the mother and three children, went to visit the maternal grandparents in Chatham. Ford had been unemployed, but obtained work at Rochester. He remained at Chatham when the mother and children returned to Edinburgh.' From this, it seems clear that our family had money difficulties, which must have placed a huge strain on a relationship already beset by problems. At this chance of work in Kent, my mother had even been willing to return to a world in which she would face her condemnatory parents, but clearly she couldn't bear it for long. I can imagine that my father would have chosen to stay with secure employment (making engine pumps), sending his money back to Breda; and that my mother would have returned to Edinburgh with us, away from the family which had never supported her, with vague plans to return once Don had settled in. However, this long-distance relationship was doomed. My mother was not a woman to sit at home quietly waiting for a man – a man who was only one in a long list.

Don Ford got himself a flat in Chatham which Breda did visit once, but arguments and 'misunderstandings' led to a less than idyllic reunion. Different reports show that the flat my Dad had secured came with a condition – he had to look after the ill old man who also lived there. Apparently, he sent a telegram to my mother in which he outlined the old man's state of health, and she arrived soon after. It would appear that there was some confusion and she thought Don had been talking about her father, my grandfather, John (although he was only 49 at the time). Breda accused my Dad of worrying her without reason and deliberately misleading her. Whatever the final words were, she headed back to Edinburgh and things went from bad to worse. 'Subsequently, Ford received disquieting reports of her conduct.' What had he been told? By whom? My mother's story always seems to have voices in the background – 'people' determining how she should be portrayed, 'people' calling in the RSSPCC, 'people' passing on 'disquieting' reports. Gossips? Busybodies? Bored neighbours? Or people genuinely concerned for the three children at the centre of all this? Given what was to happen to me in later years, and the amazing ability of all adults around me to turn a blind eye, I am more open to the explanation of a meddlesome community whose involvement went no further than telling tales and messing up lives, but that is something I'll never truly know. Whatever the reason, my father 'made a surprise visit to her house in Edinburgh, and found several women occupying the premises as well as the mother – who was drunk. After a hysterical scene, the mother walked out with her women friends and was not seen again.'

Added to this was the fact that all three of us children were in the City Hospital with whooping cough (which, in my case, turned into pneumonia). I can't imagine what it was like for us or how we dealt with the fact that we had no idea what was going on. What must it have been like for us to come out of hospital to find our father at home ready to care for us but no sign of our mother?

But why did she finally go? Why that time rather than any of the others? Was it because of the violence I have been told about in snippets? Was it because she could finally take no more whispering and name-calling? Was it because she had a dream to follow which didn't involve us? One thing is clear – they fought, she left, I never saw my mother again and my life would change forever.

℈

Frances, Simon and I were 'duly returned' to my Dad, who must have specifically requested this, given that I was the only one biologically linked to him. Frances went to school; Simon and I went to a day nursery. It all seems relatively straightforward.

Then comes the line that chills me to the bone.

In the middle of a page, in the middle of our story, come 12 words that I know alter everything.

'*Ford engaged a young girl, aged 17, to look after the home.*'

That's her.

That's Helen.

She's in my life. She's sneaked in without me noticing.

I want to scream at those words as soon as I read them. Get out! Get her out now and maybe, just maybe, it can all work out fine. They're just words, but they are condemning me as I read them. I know what's going to come. I know what's going to happen. Where was I when my father asked a teenage neighbour to help out? Was I playing at nursery? Was I in his arms? Did she see me? Did she hate me straight away?

Whatever my Dad asked her to do didn't really work out. He tried for a few months to raise us all before deciding it was too much. I can't help thinking that a woman on her own in those days, without the same ability to work and earn, would have struggled on for longer, so why couldn't a man keep trying, keep the family together, such as it was? When did my Dad decide the cutoff point had been reached? Maybe he had a date in mind, maybe we pushed him to breaking point. Whatever happened, whatever prompted him, we were going to be packed off to a home.

ॐ

Haldane House had opened in 1946 as a home for boys of school age, and by 1957 it was a mixed home. It finally closed its doors 23 years later when children were moved to The Tower in Edinburgh. The notion of a children's home probably conjures up particular images for people, images of cruelty and neglect, or of orphans desperately seeking a family. My experience was a quite different matter. My time at Haldane House was happy, and I was never mistreated or ill-used. The place was quite anonymous – it didn't necessarily indulge children or treat them as precious little individuals – but I was safe. Soon I would have changed my life for the one I had at Haldane House at any price.

The very fact that I was taken in by Barnardo's may confuse some people – I wasn't an orphan, I wasn't destitute, but my father clearly felt he could no longer cope. I have often wondered how things would have turned out if only one part of the jigsaw had been put in a different place. What if Don Ford had just been looking after me, not my half-siblings? What if he had moved from Edinburgh to start afresh when Breda left? What if he had never asked Helen to 'help'? What if Barnardo's had refused to take us, or refused to accept me, and encouraged my father to keep trying, to keep plodding along and doing the best he could?

But Haldane House did take me and my story went on.

My mother was gone but she had left debts of hundreds of pounds, which Don Ford was paying off on her behalf. He paid £2.12s.6d for a fireplace, sink unit and other furniture, with a total of £300 still to clear. She had also managed to run up debts with five different clothing clubs, with about £120 of arrears. On top of that, my father also had outstanding gas, electricity, plumbing and tradesmen's bills to pay – and everything had to come from the £8.9s he made each week as a bus driver, and the 18s of family allowance for all three children.

Barnardo's records show that officials thought well of my father trying to cope with such a financial and familial burden. Haldane House representatives contacted members of my family when they could, but Breda's mother, Mary, made it clear that she was unwilling to help, given that she believed her own daughter to be a lost cause – 'beyond redemption' as the records state. Clearly, if the mother was such a loss, the children were believed to be tainted as well.

From what I can gather, the decision to place us in Haldane House was a joint one between my father and the RSSPCC, represented by a Mr Smith. On the original application, it is emphasised that, although Breda was a lapsed Catholic, none of her three children had been baptised. Rectifying that became a condition of our acceptance.

Before we were finally accepted into the home, officials interviewed the matron at Pilrig Nursery to determine what sort of children Simon and myself were. The report glows with references to my father. 'Miss Robertson has a great admiration for the father whom she has watched rushing home in between shifts, doing without breakfast sometimes to take the children to the nursery, and who seems devoted to the children.' Miss Robertson clearly approved of my father and his efforts – and she was the only person who noticed that things were not quite right. Helen – the girl who was 'helping out' – was not to her liking. 'The girl who sometimes brings them does not appeal to Miss Robertson who thought her unsuitable and rather unstable. On one occasion, the girl brought the children to the Nursery at 7.30am and left them in the charge of the cleaners until the opening time of 8.50am.' But Miss Robertson's words would never be heard, and it would be a long time before anyone would ever pay any heed to the 'instability' of the 17-year-old girl who was to become so trusted with our little lives.

By the beginning of January 1961, everything was in place for our move to Haldane House. I was 18 months old and, apparently, a responsive child 'with a happy smile', placid, able to get on with everyone. In other words, I was normal.

Certainly, I was acceptable to Dr Barnardo's Homes, and on 3 January 1961, they wrote: 'We feel that we would be justified in taking over the care of these three children.' For their help, my father would have to pay eight shillings per week each for

Frances and Simon, ten shillings per week for me, and agree to our immediate baptism. He signed a contract to say that we would be raised Protestant, that Barnardo's could place us in any occupation it deemed proper, and that he would take us back at any time if asked to do so. The Scottish Chief Executive Officer then wrote to a Mr Roberts at Haldane House. The letter reads like a formal note of introduction, and the details provided are scant – our names and dates of birth are virtually all that identify us. Mr Roberts is told that my mother has 'deserted' and that Don Ford cannot – 'of course' – care for us. 'This little family', as he calls us in his communications, will be arriving within two days.

My life then continues within pages and pages of documentation. Rarely is my middle name spelled correctly; never is my mother referred to as Breda. But the same words are always applied to me: *good*; *happy*; *affectionate*; *warm*; *normal*; *friendly*; *plays well with her dolly*; *steady in her mood*; *lovable child*; *very popular*. These are words I would soon have difficulty applying to my life – and to read them, even now, feels alien. Was that really me? In some ways, it would be easier to see me marked by records from the past. If the foolscap sheets said I was *ugly*; *miserable*; *awkward*; *difficult* then I could at least understand, partially, what Helen would soon see to hate in me. But a happy, affectionate toddler? Why did she want to break that child? When did she decide that was going to be her project?

ॐ

It is clear that while we were in Haldane House, my father's relationship with Helen went from strength to strength. No longer did he have three young children to worry about, nor the daily logistics of ferrying them to and from school and nursery. Helen, who had been asked to help out while we were all living at Easter Road, soon became part of his life, even without us. By

November 1961, she was writing to Barnardo's on my father's behalf when there were queries about maintenance payments. Notes from 'Miss Helen Gourlay of 31 Easter Road' made it clear that she was my Dad's new co-habitee. One month later, on 11 December 1961, they were married. One letter from my files states that my father and new stepmother were visited by a Barnardo's representative. She was pregnant by that time with their first child, and it is clear that financial problems were already causing trouble between them.

Over the next year or so, many letters and reports showed that money was tight, even more so after my father became unwell. At one point, Barnardo's grew concerned that my father had not been visiting us in Haldane House. The Chief Executive Officer then asked a caseworker to go to the Easter Road flat where my father lived and see 'if there was any trouble'. The follow-up letter from this visit states: 'Father was ill and had a major operation when he was off work for three months. This, together with much debt left by the children's mother, caused him to fall behind with his payments to us.' The report goes on: 'He apologised for causing us trouble and was sorry not to have visited the children and hopes to do so again. Although he is happily married, he is rather disappointed that his wife has never suggested having the three children home for good.'

This letter tells me a lot. I'm not sure exactly how the authorities worked out that Don and Helen were 'happily married' – they probably simply assumed that a recently-wed couple expecting their first baby fell into that category – but there is obviously tension building up, even at this early stage. As far back as I can remember, Helen always complained about money. Given how much she would prove to hate my mother, the continuing existence of debts left behind by my father's ex-partner would have, no doubt, enraged her. I wonder whether my father's decreased visits to see us all were truly down to his unspecified illness, or whether Helen was already applying pressure for him to cut back on contact with me and my two half-siblings. It was a strange and complicated setup from the outset. I'm sure she wanted nothing to do with us, no reminders of our mother, yet she was living in a flat which, technically, belonged to her now-departed rival. My father must have said something, on the quiet, to the Barnardo's representative when they visited Easter Road. He must have found the space, the privacy, to mention that his new 19-year-old wife wasn't quite so forth-coming about restoring the whole family as he had hoped.

A hand-scrawled note from the caseworker on a Barnardo's letter in November 1962 says: 'I think we should keep in touch in the hope that restoration might follow, although one can understand a wife not being anxious to take on 3 children all by different fathers and she only 19. I wonder if she knows the real facts.' Again, Helen is being given the benefit of the doubt – good, kind, teenage Helen who is having to take on so much. Perhaps Barnardo's were more suspicious of my father – by asking whether Helen knew 'the real facts', maybe they are referring to the different paternity of each of us. Perhaps they thought Don hadn't told Helen he was not the father of Frances and Simon because, by keeping quiet, he would have more chance of getting her to take us all back. That, in turn, makes sense only if he actively wanted all three of us, a scenario that seems valid only if it was the flat Frances's father had left which was the real object of his intentions. It is all very confusing, and so long ago that I will never know the truth. Even now, even after years of trying to pick it all apart, I haven't uncovered everything.

The people at Barnardo's were good to me while I lived there. I visited other families and played with their children at weekends. I always had enough to eat and was kept safe and well. I was not one of those children who now claim that their years in a children's home were marked by abuse and terror. That would not come to me until I left institutional care – until I was in the heart of a family unit.

I don't remember very much about the home – partly because I was so young, but also because very little happened. We weren't treated badly, but there was no affection, no softness. I do recall one worker, though. I'm not sure whether she lived in or not. I called her Scratchy Morag. I have memories of climbing up on her, curling up on her lap, and getting a cuddle every so often. She always wore these big, fluffy mohair sweaters, and as a little girl, the scratchiness stayed in my mind. I always felt itchy after Morag had cuddled me, and she is the only one I remember giving a name to, much less an affectionate nickname.

There was little love at Haldane House, only practicality. However, I now know that there was some contact from my family, about which I knew nothing at the time. It was from my maternal grandmother, who had only ever shown interest in my elder half-sister Frances. Maybe the fact that Frances had a more 'respectable' father appealed to my Granny (ignoring the fact that he was so much older than Breda and a family member who chose to do a runner after his daughter was born). Whatever the reason, Granny Curran contacted Barnardo's in March 1963, just a few months before I was returned to my father.

The handwritten letter from her home in Chatham reads:

Dear Sir –

I am writing on the interest of my daughters children as I have never heard or seen my daughter since you called on me during February 1961. I would like to know if they are still in the home. I would like you to let me know as for some time before they were put in the home Frances who is now seven year's old was staying with me for some time. I would like a welfare officer to call and let me know something about her.

Sincerely your's –
Mrs J. Curran

A letter was then sent from the Regional Executive Officer of

Barnardo's to our caseworker, in which news of us all is requested. It is from this point that our 'little family', with its complicated history, generates a lot of correspondence. The Regional Executive Officer believed that 'it would be helpful if we could have a little more news to send on to Mrs Curran ... We should also be interested to know whether Mr Ford has continued to keep in touch with the children, and if so, whether his wife has shown any interest.'

Within two days, there is an answer from the Chief Executive Officer.

Re: Frances Cummings, Simon Robertson
and Donna Ford – at Haldane House

Thank you for your letter ... concerning these children.
All the children are well and attractive little people, especially small Donna.
The father is not keeping much in touch these days, and now that he is married to a very young wife, and they have a newly born baby of their own, I think it is really expecting rather too much to expect him to continue to take responsibility for these three.
I am, therefore, proposing to board them out as soon as we can find a suitable home.

Another letter, almost two weeks later tells her:

They say that little Donna is especially charming.
Unfortunately, neither of their parents seems able to keep in very close touch with the children and we are therefore planning to find a suitable home where they can be fostered, so that this will give them the opportunity of growing up in the environment of a normal happy home, where they will receive every loving care and attention.

My Granny was then sent a letter giving her the information that we were all at Haldane House and 'quite settled'. She was also asked if she could write to us 'as they would be delighted to have news from their own grannie'. To my knowledge, I never received any such letter or any cheery granny-news. In some ways, that doesn't bother me – it seems unlikely that the woman who was so cold to Breda would have been much of a force for good in my life, and she was obviously only bothered about Frances. There is, however, a tiny voice which asks whether she would have seen through Helen if she had met her. Would she have stood up for me? Would she have prevented Helen from plunging me into hell? But that is all wishful thinking. No, I am much more drawn to the few phrases which give me the colour of my own being at that time.

The quotes which tell me that I was 'attractive' and 'charming' knock me for six. Who is this child? Who is this normal toddler? To have such phrases, such images, compounded by the never-realised promise of a foster home where I would receive 'every loving care and attention' is nothing short of fantasy. What would have become of me? Would I have fulfilled the promise implicit in those early Barnardo's reports? Medical reports confirm the normality – I get measles, I get colds. I develop 'normally', I act 'normally', I am 'normal for age'. I am a 'likeable child developing well'.

> *Donna is the youngest and has not yet started school but is a bright wee girl.*
>
> *Her habits are clean.*
>
> *The health of the children has given no cause for concern.*
>
> *The children mix well with the staff and other members of our family and are well behaved. They are polite and very anxious to please.*
>
> *They are affectionate children.*

Within a few months of my grandmother's enquiries, and the Barnardo's reports that Helen was not showing much – if any – interest in us, things changed for some reason. By September 1963, Helen had become 'very anxious' to have us restored to her care. 'She and Mr Ford have been visiting regularly and hope to visit every third Sunday which is Mr Ford's Sunday off.' By this time, Gordon had been born (in November 1962), and was a 'great success with the children'. In retrospect, this seems perfectly natural. Children tend to like babies, and, on top of that, we were seeing the woman who would be our eventual 'carer' in a maternal role. As she sat there with a baby, dandling him on her lap, cuddling and kissing him, who could blame me – and presumably my two half-siblings – from dreaming that one day soon we would receive the same care, the same delayed surrogate mother's attentions?

This image of Helen Gourlay, now Helen Ford, was attractive not just to me – to us – but to the authorities as well. The reports speak admiringly of the small basement flat in which she and my father lived, and the fact that some internal renovations and decorating were ongoing, as well as the way in which she was the one dealing with my mother's debts. And, I admit, on paper it does look good.

Although she is only 20, she seems quite a remarkable girl – determined to keep a good home and make a happy home for the whole family. She has done wonders with the various debts and keeps her 'books' most methodically so that she knows exactly how she stands financially. She says she could not be happier and she and her husband get on well together.

I wish that the Helen who seems so together in those reports had stayed. I wonder what happened? Knowing what was to become of me, what she was going to turn my life into – I think about whether she changed or whether she was putting on an act for the authorities. It seems fanciful that she would make such an effort just to get me back, but what other options are there? Did it all get too much once I was there? Did she regret having us 'restored'? Did something resurface from her past which made her – or turned her back into – the monster who ruined my childhood?

I don't have the answers to these questions and I never will. However, that Helen is the one I was given to just a few months later. The reports stand – but so do the earlier ones in which concerns were raised about her lack of responsibility when we still lived with my father.

I was to be the first of my mother's three children to return to Don and Helen Ford – naturally enough, given that I was the only one who had a blood link to the man taking us in. In preparation for this restoration, the official visits to, and reports about, the flat in Easter Road intensified. The request for restoration was made in March 1964, and the paper trail multiplies from that point. The same facts come out time and time again – the flat is tiny; there is a lot of debt; the authorities wish to keep a close eye on the situation. In one letter, of 12 March 1964, it is stated that:

> *The mother has been seen in Edinburgh on two occasions, but Mr Ford does not think she is still here. Since she left the children she has been sought by Family Allowance because she took the book. The RSSPCC tried to find her – also without success.*
>
> *Mr Ford is to consult X – a friend of the mother – either to ask X to see us, or to try and get word to the mother that we would like to see her.*

The thought that my mother might have been in Edinburgh twice, so close, chills me. Did she come back to try and find out what had happened to us, or was she just back to see friends without any thought for the children she left behind? The fact that she kept the Family Allowance book also bothers me – it didn't matter in terms of the money because another document confirms that my father was receiving the allowance (in fact, it paid for Frances, Simon and me to be kept by Barnardo's). What bothers me is whether she kept it because it was one of the few official documents she had which may have allowed her to prove her claim to us if she did intend to come back. The elusive 'X' never did come through, as far as I know, and Breda never reappeared.

With no Breda, and no reason to keep us away from Easter Road, meetings and visits continued. On 19 June, our case-worker made a final trip to Edinburgh to see where I would be living. It had been agreed that all the stops would be pulled out to get me there before August when the Scottish school year starts. I was to begin school for the very first time – from my home. Barnardo's had a few more requests – as well as trying to trace my mother, they were concerned about who owned the Easter Road property. Don Ford said that he would attempt to contact Frances's father – Robert Cummings – to have the bond transferred to him as guardian. He doesn't seem to have been traced at that point – and I have no idea how that ended.

On 8 July 1964, I was given my final progress report from Barnardo's.

Donna is a very healthy little girl.

Her habits are clean.

She is a bright child, with I should think, a very good I.Q.

Affectionate and kindly disposed to others she mixes well with adults and children.

Her mental and physical progress has been satisfactory and I feel the future for Donna is bright. Strong foundations have been well and truly laid.

When I arrived at Haldane House I had little more than my milk tokens, my vitamin token book and my medical card. And a promise. On my admission letter is one phrase that strikes me. Alongside 'reason for removal' is that one word which keeps coming back through reports and records and caseworker correspondence: ***restoration***. I was not there indefinitely; I was there until my father found his feet. I would be restored to him, he would be restored to me, and my life would survive this little blip.

On one of the final documents I have are the words that haunt me to this day. As I made my world around Haldane House, as I played and laughed and grew, I was being watched. The conclusion? *'The youngest member of our family and the darling of all.'*

Not quite.

Chapter Three

∾

GOING HOME

July 1964

I WAS GOING HOME. Home, home, home! To 31 Easter Road, a Victorian tenement block in Edinburgh. The whole Easter Road area was a community in itself. Although only a few minutes' bus ride from the centre of the city, Princes Street, it was a completely different world. One phrase for Easter Road would be, I'm sure, 'traditional'. In all honesty, it was run-down, working class and dirty.

Buses went up and down the main road to virtually everywhere in the city, and the shops lining either side of the thoroughfare sold absolutely everything. There was Rankin's the fruiterers, where produce was always put in brown paper bags, twirled over at each corner before you paid. There was a stream of grocer's shops where you could buy cheap booze, single fags and true-life crime magazines. There were second-hand shops, and shops with their own 'savings club' where clothes could be paid for on a weekly basis and no one would ask about the exorbitant prices, grateful to get anything on tick. There were tenements towering above every step you took. At the bottom of the road was the entrance to the Hibernian football ground, which made every other Saturday afternoon feel as if Easter Road were the centre of the universe.

The noise was constant. The smell of bus fumes and never-ending life was overwhelming. There was usually a fight going on somewhere – and not just at chucking-out time. There was always a group of women with prams having a gossip. There was always somebody's husband staggering up the street at some time of day, facing a chicken run of shouts and laughter. Of course, I had lived there before, but I had left when I was little more than 18 months old. Returning to the flat my Dad now shared with his new wife, Helen, I was the grand old age of five and ready to take it all in.

At that stage of childhood, there are things that always stay with you. Everyone remembers a favourite story, toy or pet. Most people recall where they lived or what their room was like, or whether they were scared of ghosts as they snuggled down for the night. I'm no different – my memories of Easter Road are etched on my brain. It's only when I look at what I remember – and why – that the childhood visions start to turn into horrors.

༄

I woke up on the morning of 8 July 1964 and knew it was a special day. I had spent the past three-and-a-half years at Haldane House, but today I was going home. My Daddy was coming for me, and when I left that day, I'd never be back. Having a Daddy and a home miles away in Edinburgh meant that I never felt I belonged at Barnardo's. I wasn't waiting to be adopted; I was just waiting to be 'restored', to go back to where I belonged.

It hadn't been easy. Don Ford was my father – but definitely not the father of my half-brother and half-sister. At this stage he was not trying to have all three of us to stay with him and his new wife and baby. As he described himself as their 'guardian', and had looked after them in the immediate period after my mother left, he had proven himself to a degree, but, as the Barnardo's records show:

this ... has ... raised all sorts of legal points and we have been
striving to contact the children's mother without success. The
maternal grandmother has not heard from her since the
children were admitted ... we propose, therefore, to restore
Donna to her father in the meantime, leaving both Frances
and Simon at Haldane House until we have cleared up any
legal points and seen as many people as we can who are
involved with these children.

It does seem as if Barnardo's were being very careful, at least on
the legal side. There is a handwritten note attached to the
document quoted above in which someone has obviously jotted
down the pertinent questions regarding this tricky situation:

1 *Who? can claim legal custody of*
    a Frances Cummings
    b Simon Robertson
    c Donna Ford
   any trace of RH Cummings –
   what efforts must be made to trace M?
   on what grounds, if any, can F's claim be resisted?
   What legal right has putative father?

So many questions – and none of them really answered in the
intervening years. My mother was being traced. No one
knew whether the fathers of Frances and Simon were around
or wanted their children. The legal rights seemed to be more
and more confusing. Only one thing was clear – I was to be
restored.

I was dressed and ready long before he arrived for me. I had
a little bag packed with my few things, and I sat by the window,
full of anticipation. This was where my life started; this was
where I would become the little girl I wanted to be. I knew that
Helen would be at Easter Road when we got there. I had already

been told that she wouldn't come with my Dad, but my five-year-old mind couldn't help thinking that this was because she would be getting things ready for me. I would be the homecoming princess. Maybe my new Mummy was decorating my bedroom. Maybe she was setting out my new toys and dollies on my bed. Maybe she was baking a cake with pink icing and sugar flowers and little silver balls for my first teatime at home. I thought about how she used to sit baby Gordon on her lap, always cuddling him, always loving him. She looked so happy with her baby; she loved him so much – imagine how delighted she would be to get a little girl to love as well!

I don't remember much about my Dad actually arriving to pick me up. The parts I do recall are similar to his previous visits with Helen. He was waiting in the 'big room' where all family meetings took place. He was dressed in his grey herringbone overcoat with shiny black shoes and a white shirt and dark tie. My Dad never went out of the house in those days without a shirt and tie. He always wanted to be presentable. His jet black hair was slicked back with Brylcreem, and his glasses looked too big on his too-small face. I walked up to him and he seemed huge – even although he was only five foot seven – because he was My Daddy and he was taking me HOME!

My father signed a sheet of paper saying that he had received all my personal belongings. While he was doing this, I waited, as I had been for some time.

I don't remember too much about the train journey home and then the bus ride in Edinburgh. It was just an assortment of transport from Haldane House onwards. I was both sad and happy – I was leaving my older sister and brother behind, the only real family I'd ever known, but I was reassured that they would be with me soon. I wasn't to know that this was the longest amount of time I would ever spend alone with my Dad for the rest of my childhood – and I would certainly never feel so carefree again.

I was looking forward to going home so much – I was sure I was going to the same sort of home I had visited when I went to stay with other families at weekends. I was sure I would be greeted by the smell of home cooking and the feeling of love. It would all be lovely. I knew that Simon and Frances would be joining us at some point in the future, and I looked forward to that – but, that day, it was just me and him. It felt perfect.

If I'd known what was in store for me, I'd have turned on my heels and ran away as fast as my skinny little legs could carry me.

 ᧔

As we arrived at the stair door of the tenement flat, I looked up at the huge building. This was it. This was home. My Dad looked down at me. 'You alright, hen?' he asked. 'Nothing to worry about,' he said, looking at my big, wide, brown eyes. 'This is where we'll all live – this is where you stay. Now, Helen might be a wee bit busy with the baby, but she's looking forward to you being here. None of us could wait to have you back. And we'll get your brother and your sister as soon as we can. You'll be fine. Just fine.' He squeezed my hand – I'd been holding on to him since we left Haldane House – and put his other hand into a pocket to take out a big latchkey. He slid it into the hole in the big door as I stared up at the number 31 etched on glass above. As soon as the door closed behind us, I could smell the people who lived there. The stink of a dozen meals being cooked at once, of people living too close to each other, of bins needing emptying, all swept up and hit me. There were echoing sounds coming from behind closed doors – behind each one was a different world to mine. I looked up at the immense stone staircase which led to each front door and seemed to stop only when it reached the sky – which entrance would be ours?

My Dad pulled me gently along the cold concrete corridor with its two-tone walls. The top half had a splattered paint effect, as if someone at some point had decided this would make all the difference to a communal stairwell. We turned past a pile of prams stacked neatly at the bottom of the staircase – how many babies lived here? I would be very grown up in a place like this, I thought. I looked up and could see the clouds through the glazed cupola – it all seemed so bright and summery that even the smells and the noises didn't matter. My excitement was building. When would we start climbing up to the sky? When would I find out which magic door led to my kingdom?

I was thrown off balance as we headed down some steps which twisted around to the left. Why were we going this way? As we went down, about four steps up from the ground, I saw a door in the wall. 'What's that, Daddy?' I asked. 'Oh, just the coal cellar,' he answered distractedly. 'Nothing important.'

Just the coal cellar.

Nothing important.

I'd remember those words – sooner rather than later.

The descent would symbolise more than the first disappointment I was to face – I was being taken into the very depths of despair.

'Why are we going down here, Daddy?' I persisted. 'Are we going to visit someone before we go up to our house?' My Dad laughed. 'This is where you live now, Donna. We live down these stairs. The basement. We all live in the basement.' I wasn't going to the stars, I wasn't heading up to the sky after all.

Once we reached the communal passageway, there was a door to the back garden – or the 'back green' as we always called it. On the right-hand side was our door, our house. My Dad opened the front door and I looked down a long corridor, or lobby, with doors along the left-hand side. The first tiny door on the left was I was told, the 'kids' bedroom' – I wasn't getting a pink hideaway to myself; I was being shoehorned into a tiny room with whichever half-siblings were going to be around. Next door was the bathroom, and straight ahead the living room. On the right-hand side of the lobby there were no doors, just a recess which was being turned into something. There was no flooring in there, just rubble, and the smell of damp and plaster permeated the entire flat.

The flat was so small that every inch of space in every room felt squeezed. In 'my' tiny room, there was one window and a fireplace, above which there was a picture of Jesus. His eyes seemed to follow me around the room, and never once did I feel He wasn't watching me. It was just a shame He never did anything to help. The bedroom was incredibly cramped as bunk beds had been crammed in alongside a cot.

A representative from Barnardo's had already been to visit and commented on the size of the flat.

> *The flat is tiny and consists of a living-room, bedroom and bathroom. Mr Ford has worked very hard altering the house to make it more manageable, i.e. putting in swing doors on the children's room because of the situation of the bunk beds; boxing in the bath and he and his brother are rewiring the house and re-decorating.*
>
> *The bedroom has new bunk beds and it was originally arranged to have two bunk-beds, but they just could not get the second one into the room. As a result the room has the top bunk for Simon and the bottom bunk for Frances and Donna meantime. Gordon's cot is also in the room, plus a dressing table and chest of drawers.*

My Dad introduced me to this minuscule, cramped environment. 'What do you think, then?' he asked, squatting down beside me. 'What do you think of your new home?' I hated it. I hated it straight away. It just wasn't what I had dreamed of, but I tried to focus on what really mattered. It wasn't a children's home, and I had my Dad and stepmother here, my new half-brother whom I hardly knew, and my other half-siblings coming to join me soon. There were places to play, and surely there would be other children in the stair to make friends with.

'It's lovely, Dad,' I answered. 'Just lovely.'

He took my hand and walked towards the living room. Again, in such a small place, one room had many functions. There was a small kitchen, or scullery, looking out on to the back green, in line with the bathroom and my bedroom. There was a fireplace in the living room which had been converted from its original Victorian splendour into a bog-standard, ugly, grey-tiled box. And the room was also Don and Helen's bedroom. A recess later housed a sofa bed, which they swapped for a double bed when Helen had her next baby. I looked around the room – I had been born there, and already it was giving me the creeps.

My memories of that first day don't really go past those few snippets – holding my Dad's hand all the time, getting the layout of 31 Easter Road, feeling disappointed, but hoping – really hoping – that it would all be perfect. I do remember that Helen paid me very little attention; there was no sign that she had indeed been looking forward to my arrival, despite what my Dad had said earlier. That didn't strike me as too odd – I would have liked a cuddle from her, but I knew she had Gordon and realised she would probably get round to me soon enough.

And she certainly did.

～

As the days and weeks went on, I realised that Helen was my day-to-day world, much more than my father. He worked while she stayed at home. He never seemed to be there, and I felt his absence. It was the long summer holiday and I was waiting to start school in late August. Some days she would let me out to play in the back green, but I had to make my own amusement.

She would never play with me, and I don't recall ever having anything of my own. Five-year-olds hold it all in their heads though – I'd lie in the long grass and sing to myself, make up stories, and dream of the perfect world I still hoped for. Most of all, I thought of Tiny Tears dolls. I had seen these toys advertised; I had witnessed other girls playing with them when I went on trips with Barnardo's – and my heart ached for one. I lay there on the grass and thought about how a Tiny Tears would make my life complete. A dolly of my own; a dolly who could cry 'real' tears, that I could dress and nurse and sing to. I could almost touch my Tiny Tears, I thought about her so much.

That first summer was, ironically, the best of my whole childhood. It may not have been much compared to other kids, but given what was waiting for me, I should have been deliriously happy. At times, Helen would take me out to visit her friends or go to the shops; looking back, I can see she was showing both me and herself off. I was the girl with the mother who had deserted her – I was unloved, abandoned and, through her goodness, Helen had rescued me from an orphanage. When we met with other people, I could see how she glowed as they praised her, and while I was part of that charade, she had a use for me.

I loved it when we did normal things, boring day-to-day chores which I had totally missed out on in Haldane House. I remember playing in the back green, with Gordon lying on a fluffy blanket decorated with a duck. Helen was there – she rarely left her golden boy – and there were other children around. The sun was shining and I was happy. I had a Daddy, an almost-Mummy, a baby and a home. I also remember holding on to the handle of the pram as Helen shopped in Easter Road. We went from one place to another. In the greengrocer's, potatoes would be weighed then slid straight off the big chrome bowl into the tattie bag that Helen held open. In Laing's the butcher's, our mince, sausages, rissoles, chopped ham and pork would be weighed then wrapped in greaseproof paper. The Co-Op was a delight with its shelves stacked high with staples, and Green Shield Stamps handed out for every purchase.

But something changed to take away even the few good times. I knew Helen had a temper, but it soon became clear to me that I couldn't do anything to prevent her outbursts. As an adult, I can see that she was always upset by the fact that I was my father's first child, and that I had created a lot of attention in his family when I was born, attention she desperately wanted for Gordon. As a child, I had no idea what was going on. She began to taunt me a lot, but I was still too young to know what was going on or even understand what she was saying.

One of her early outbursts happened one day when I was standing behind her in the pantry. There had never been any loving contact between us – she never hugged me or snuggled me in for stories – but the fact of her coldness hadn't quite got through to me yet. When I first arrived I wanted so much for her to like me. I wanted it so much that I just didn't know what to do. I'd look at her bouncing Gordon on her knee, singing him songs, kissing him, and I wanted some of that. I did like Gordon when he was little: it was only when he got older and Helen turned him into her ally, telling tales, making up stories that I realised we would never even be friends. I often hung around her, thinking that basic proximity would result in some of the affection she lavished on Gordon rubbing off on me. On this particular day, maybe I was standing too close, maybe I made her feel claustrophobic, but she wheeled round suddenly. 'Get away,' she hissed. 'Get away from me, you snivelling little bastard.' I stood stock still. I didn't even know what the word meant. Her voice got higher and louder. 'Didn't you hear me? Are you deaf and thick as well as ugly? Get away, you bastard child! Get away from me.' I may not have understood what the word stood for, but I knew enough to get away.

From then on, the poky bedroom became a place where I was sent, not somewhere I would choose to go. After that first

incidence of verbal abuse, it was as if the floodgates had opened.
She rarely stopped. I had been naïve enough to think that the
worst thing was being ignored – well, now I was getting plenty of
attention and it was horrible. She didn't taunt me when my Dad
was there, and she made it quite clear that I wasn't to mention it
to him either. As soon as he came home from work, she would
start making little comments about how difficult I was, how
awkward, how unhelpful, what a saint she was for putting up
with me – and, instead of being the good, lovely Daddy I was
desperate for, he believed every word of it. He'd tell me to be
good, to help Helen, to realise how lucky I was and not to make
things difficult, but he never once asked me if it was true. I was
so little that I couldn't have made complicated arguments for and
against our relative positions, but I knew right from wrong, and
I knew when things were unjust.

When Helen's temper flared, she would scream at me to go to
my room and then bark out some more orders. 'Sit on the bed!
Get your legs straight out! Put your arms straight down by your
sides!' I would have to stay like that for as long as she determined
was appropriate. It was agony. My back ached; my limbs ached;
I wasn't allowed to cry; I wasn't allowed to move. I honestly
thought that if I even blinked too much, she would know and I
would be punished even more. There were a few variations. Some
days, there would be new additions: 'Take off your clothes! Keep
your vest and pants on! Face the wall! Don't look at the wall!
Look at the ceiling!' The punishment was always for nothing; it
was always for something she had decreed to be a flouting of the
rules, even although they were rules of which I had never even
been made aware.

As time went on, more punishments for more unspoken rules
emerged. I would be sent into the lobby where the brick recess
was still standing unfinished. My Dad and Uncle Alex were
allegedly making this space into a little room, but, like most of
my Dad's projects, it never really came to anything beyond the

initial wrecking. It was so tiny and odd-shaped that I doubt he could have done anything to it with the best will in the world, so the rubble remained, the bricks stayed exposed and the stink of damp was there constantly. It became another focus of Helen's increasing hatred of me. 'Get in there, bastard child,' she would snarl. 'Get in there. Face the wall. Don't move or I'll know about it. Then you'll have it coming. Ugly little bastard.' I didn't know what was 'coming' but it always seemed that what she implicitly threatened me with would be even worse than what I was enduring. Hours spent in a hole in the wall staring at nothing as I got colder and ached more, and felt the hunger rise through me until I shook, seemed preferable to Helen's next stage of punishment, whatever it turned out to be.

If the damp recess wasn't to my stepmother's liking, and the bedroom had lost its attraction, then the bathroom always came in useful. It was a very long, narrow room with a bath, toilet and sink. There was a pulley above the bath, and I remember having to let it down on its squeaky runners to hang up wet washing. There was a high ceiling and it was always freezing. Helen would decide which of her favourite options would be chosen that day. 'Stand in the bath,' she told me the first time I was sent to that room. 'Take all your things off apart from your vest and knickers and stand there, bastard, just stand there.' I did as I was told. She pushed her face close up to mine. 'You'll stand there until you learn your lesson. Don't move. Don't breathe. Don't sing or talk to yourself. Just stand there.' And I did. Other times, I'd be told to stand by the toilet, but the same routine held. No moving. No sound. No indication that it was anything other than what I deserved.

That was my life. I was five years old. I had a father who saw nothing. I had a stepmother who hated me. I had a stepbrother who was turning into a pawn for his mother. There was no sign that my half-brother and half-sister were going to be arriving any time soon. I was always cold, always hungry. I was never hugged, never loved. I was already learning degradation and meaningless punishment for imaginary transgressions that were never explained.

I was home.

Chapter Four

THE LITTLE WITCH

1964–1965

DESPITE THE AWFUL THINGS Helen was already doing to me, that first summer at Easter Road is one of the few times I remember having happy moments. A lot of the early days – before the recess, before the beatings – were spent being introduced to other members of the family, particularly on my Dad's side. These family visits were the only time I ever saw him properly – the rest of our moments together were fleeting, when he was rushing out to work, or listening to Helen's criticisms of me. However, when we went to see his family, I got to be with him for much longer. I was carted around, shown off, and that seemed much more in line with what I had expected to happen when I first left Barnardo's.

I don't know what to make of those relatives now. There were lots of them – the Fords were a sprawling bunch – but for all their friendliness, they were never really there for me. They saw me come back into the family, they knew my history – and that was enough. These people flit through my memory now as characters in a play, a play that is my life, but they're just walk-on parts – and perhaps that's how I appeared to them as well. I was just wee Donna, Don's daughter, the one who should be so very grateful to that nice young lassie Helen for taking her back in when my own evil mother had deserted her.

Uncle George and Auntie Valerie were two of the first I met. They lived in a 'nice house' in Clermiston, on the north-west side of the city. Edinburgh, like all other places I suppose, was very clear in its delineation of what constituted 'nice' people and 'nice' places. Cleanliness and not bothering others had a lot to do with it, but your address and the proximity of green spaces and fewer pubs really got a family up a few notches. George was one of my Dad's brothers. I remember he was older and greyer than Don. He wore glasses and always had a very serious air about him, as if he was permanently worried about something he couldn't voice. He and his wife had two children – Gordon and little Valerie – and, to me, they ticked all the boxes: a proper family with Mum, Dad and kids who weren't sent to a home.

Uncle Alex was very different. My main memory of him is of a man who had a great sense of fun and an air of mischief about him. He was married and had children too, but it is Alex himself – not as a Dad or a husband but as an individual – who is burned in my mind. He was one of those people who makes everyone smile just by being there, a real joker. Others were always happy to see him, always laughing when he was around. Most surprisingly for me, my Dad changed when he was with that brother. From always seeming weary, and carrying the burdens of the world, he became a happy young man who would go out and enjoy a beer, have a joke, be *normal*. Our home life made my Dad miserable, even I could see that. Helen was always shouting at him or narking about me. We never had enough money, so she wanted him to do as much overtime or shift work as possible – of course, that also helped her in that he wasn't around to see how she treated me. She moaned that she couldn't afford to buy the things she wanted, that we had less nice stuff in the house than other people, that she didn't have the clothes all her friends could parade about in. This confused me because Helen did always seem to get what she wanted. When we went to the local shops, she generally had enough money for a lipstick or something sparkly, but, to my Dad, she constantly pleaded poverty. He must have been tired, and home offered no respite. She was at him when he left for work, and she was waiting for him when he got back. He was immediately given a list of things I had done during the day – most of them created and based around being 'evil' or looking at Helen 'funny' – and berated for bringing me back into their lives. Helen would shout at him to work on the alcove, to do things around the house, to help out with neighbours she had promised his assistance to. The man never got a moment's peace. But when we went on visits he changed, and I felt the benefit as much as anyone.

Uncle Alex and his family lived in Burntisland, a coastal town on the Firth of Forth. They lived near the 'Bin' – a law, or a hill that sits in the centre of the town, and which you can see from the other side of the Firth of Forth. I can remember always visiting them in summer, and only ever for the day. In those days, kids were generally sent out to play while the adults stayed in the house. Burntisland was a small place when I was little, and everyone seemed to know everyone else. Even today it has a population of only about six thousand, and people from Edinburgh still see it as an ideal place for a day trip. To me, it was a place of fun – I loved the trip there; I loved going to the beach and the parks; I loved the fairground even though we didn't have the money to do any of the things other families were enjoying.

When I got a couple of years older and Simon and Frances had been staying with us for a while, we could pretend to be famous in Burntisland. My cousin, one of Uncle Alex's daughters, was going out with one of the sons of the man who owned Macari's, the ice-cream shop – and in that convoluted relationship, we saw our claim to fame. Whenever we passed the shop, whenever we threw a few words at any other kids playing outside, we'd loudly declare that we were 'related' to them. And didn't it make us feel grand! By the end of any visit, we had completely convinced ourselves – but no one else – that we owned the entire shop and café. The irony was that we couldn't even afford a single cone between the three of us.

My Dad also had a younger sister whom we would visit regularly. Auntie Madge was the baby of the whole family. Helen always referred to her as 'the spinster', although it was a long time before I found out what that meant. It always sounded like an insult coming from Helen, but I don't think Madge would have seen it as such. She always liked things just right, and was quite set in her ways, despite being younger than her siblings. She was particularly neat and tidy, and had quite precise manners. Appearance was everything to Auntie Madge and I remember her clothes very clearly. She wore smart, woollen, Chanel-type suits, with nylon turtle-neck sweaters, flat patent leather sensible shoes with matching handbag, and a hat pinned 'just so'. Madge always had perfectly coiffed permed curls, a bit in the Irish mammy style, and delicate glasses. Her pearls were a permanent fixture, and I can still see her pulling on her gloves one finger at a time. She had a sickly sweet smell of foundation and perfume, combined with the air of being extremely prim and proper. Madge went to church regularly and was a Girl Guide leader. Whenever we went to visit her, I had a sense of something different, a different way of being that was very correct and absolutely unwavering. All of this made her so different from her brothers that it was hard to place them all in the same family.

Until you met Granny Ford.

༄

Granny Ford was the original family matriarch. She ruled the Fords, and no one would ever dare dispute anything she said to her face. Of course, Helen would have the last laugh in that department, but to her children, Granny Ford was the woman who mattered. She was tiny with a smiley face and grey curly hair. Round and warm, she often cuddled us when we went to visit. I clearly remember the smell of her cooking, and the way she always had something to be getting on with in the kitchen. She was always busy and ready to be working, with a floral apron tied around her, hankie in one pocket, sweetie in the other. Whenever I think about her now, I can hear the ticking of her cuckoo clock. Her bedroom smelled of lavender and the living room of coal. She was the kind of granny I would like to have known better, but she died when I was still very young, and Auntie Madge stepped into her shoes as the head female in the family. I often wonder whether I would have been able to go to my Granny when things got really bad. When Helen started to abuse me to the extent that I could see no end to it, would I have found an ally, even an escape route, if Granny Ford had been alive? All of that is just dreaming, wondering 'what if?', but I do think that she was a woman who would have laid down the law, and expected others to abide by it – perhaps she would have changed my life if she had lived longer.

I still think back to her tiny house, so warm and comforting, nestled under the railway bridge at Ashley Terrace. I never went there with Helen, only with my Dad on the number 44 bus. I didn't pay many visits as she died before I was eight or nine, and I can't remember her ever visiting our house, but what I do remember of Granny Ford is all nice – and those memories mean a lot in a childhood with precious little niceness. I recall when she died my father telling me she had fallen over and bumped her head. I never went to the funeral, and the only time I spoke to my Dad about Granny Ford was on the days when he'd been told by Helen to take the kids out. Sometimes, when my Dad wasn't at work, Helen would go on at him to take us all on a day's outing: this would often be to Holyrood Park or around the streets right up to Princes Street, the Mound, down the Bridges and along Forrest Road. He'd tell us stories of Greyfriars Bobby and show us his own postal route as he was now working as a postman. Often I'd be stopped from going, but on the times I did, I hung on to his every word as we'd walk around the streets and he'd point things out en route. On the very rare occasions when I would get time on my own with Dad, I would try to talk to him. When he wasn't around Helen he was a much kinder man. He'd talk a bit about Granny Ford and about his own father.

On trip days, Helen would claim she needed to 'get on with things' in peace. I remember a few of the occasions I was made to stay back as, according to Helen, I'd been bad. I was then made to clean the house, scrubbing the floors with a wooden brush and carbolic soap, and sweeping the carpets with the broom. I would have been only five or six years old at the time. Helen would get me to trample the blankets in the bath then wring them out, twisting to get the excess water out, then hanging them out on the washing rope in the back green. Helen also loved to get me to clean the bathroom, making sure I stuck my hand right down the toilet and cleaned and scrubbed every part of it around the rim and down the back, whacking my head on the toilet rim if I didn't do it to her satisfaction.

No matter how many trips or visits we went on, no matter how many relatives I was reintroduced to, there remained one harsh reality. I always had to go back 'home'. And in that 'home' was the one character who is etched in my mind, to this day, more vividly than all the others put together.

Helen.

෴

Physically, she was a product of her times. Although I have seen her recently in court looking like a nondescript middle-aged woman, it is the Helen of the 1960s who still haunts my dreams and takes me back to Easter Road. Her shoulder-length hair was a characterless brown. During the day, if she was just going about her business with no visitors, she would scrape it back off her face in a greasy ponytail. But when it was a day of note – a party, a night out or friends coming round – she would spend hours getting it just right. I would watch her as she curled it, or teased it into a beehive, or backcombed it until it couldn't move. Every few seconds, more hairspray would be applied – her favourites were Bel-Air and Elnett – strong, overpowering, noxious goo which would fill the room and signify that Helen was Going Out. Sometimes, she would tell me that I could help. When I was just starting my time with her at Easter Road, this was presented to me almost as a treat and, equally, I tried to accept it as such. She'd pass me the spindly comb and I'd try so hard to mould her hair into something attractive. I didn't mind to begin with because she was quiet and still throughout the charade. However, as time went on, I couldn't bear to be so close to her, and the travesty of doing such a normal task for a woman who made my life hell was just another slap on the face. In the early days, I would stand on an upturned washing basket or pile of old newspapers and brush and brush and brush and brush. I would take big, round, prickly rollers from a basket and carefully place them in her straggly locks, or I would try my hardest to curl the ends and flick them up in the latest fashion.

However, there was only so much you could do to make Helen look good. Her attempts at a hairdo were the start of the ritual, but she was always going to be dragged down by her specs and her teeth. The glasses were similar to the ones Deirdre in *Coronation Street* used to wear – great lumps of plastic on a pearlised frame with a silver flash on each arm. They dominated her face, and made any attempt at glamour quite ridiculous. Mind you, they were nothing compared to her teeth. Helen's 'falsies' would click as she talked, and it always seemed to me that she had a constant fight on her hands keeping them in. I used to be convinced that they were trying to escape, and I was mesmerised by her mouth, by the clicking, and by the hope that, one day, they would simply fly out of her mouth and she would have to shut up.

Combined with the clicky false teeth, the 'Deirdre' specs and the never-quite-right beehive was a fashion sense which always seemed a bit out of kilter as well. She loved miniskirts. In those days, it didn't really matter if your legs were up to it or not; if fashion decreed you wore something that made you look awful, you just had to go along with things. Her favourites were checked and woolly, and she liked to pair them with skinny-fit nylon jumpers. I remember Helen's legs a lot, presumably because I was so small, and I can vividly recall that, no matter how thick the American Tan tights she wore, you could still always see the mottled skin creeping through. We used to call it 'fireside tartan', where women's legs took on a blotchy effect that showed they loved sitting too close to the fire even more than they loved the latest style.

While she was indoors, Helen always wore her 'baffies', or slippers, and I have this image of her from the feet up. She was tall, or seemed so to me, almost as tall as my Dad (although he was a bit of a shortie). The baffies – which smelled and were falling apart – led to the thick American Tan tights, which showed off her fireside tartan legs right up to her short woolly miniskirt, into which was tucked a nylon, static-filled jumper. Her hands would play host to lots of gold rings with big stones – she loved fake amber jewellery – and, above the blue eyeshadow and eyeliner she loved, it was all topped off with one of her hairdos, or a conglomeration of curlers with a satin headscarf on top, tied under her chin, if she had to nip out to the shops.

All of this, all of the physical presence of Helen, is still with me. I know what else there is – I know what she was planning, what she would eventually do, but sometimes it is only by picking it apart in small pieces that I can put it together again. What did my stepmother look like? What did she wear? All of this can be approached in a way that makes sense to me, in a way that I can't really apply to the physical, mental and sexual cruelty which was already building up.

୬

The flat itself at Easter Road was damp and permanently cold. There was nearly always a coal fire lit, which Helen would constantly prod with a poker. The fire seemed to be on the verge of calling it a day at any given time, so the poker always had to be kept there, always at hand, and always white hot. One day, when I was still only five, Helen threw the poker down. As usual I didn't know specifically what I had done to annoy her. Maybe I'd said something; maybe I'd been singing; maybe I'd been staring at her clicky false teeth. She got up from her knees with rage burning in her eyes. I started to shake as she leapt over to me. 'Come here! Come here, you little witch!' she screamed. She grabbed me by my hair and forced me down by the fireside. 'Kneel there,' she hissed. 'And just you wait ...'

As I got on my knees before her, she reached out for the poker which was still burning from poking the fire a few seconds earlier. 'Put your hands out,' she commanded. 'What?' I whimpered. 'Put your hands out in front of you!' she roared. I stretched out my skinny arms, keeping my palms downwards. 'Up!' she shouted. 'Get your hands up!' I turned my palms to face her and she began lowering the poker down towards them. It came so slowly. Every inch, every part of an inch, that brought it closer meant I could feel the heat moving nearer. My tiny, shaking hands knew that this could really hurt. I would never have touched the poker on my own – I knew it was dangerous – so to have Helen bring it so close could mean only one thing – she wanted to hurt me, and she wanted to hurt me really badly this time. It was coming down closer and closer.

'Please, Helen, please ...' I started to cry. It was against my better judgement – even at that age – to show any sign of breaking down in front of her. I don't know if it was because it might make her even more angry, or whether I just wanted to feel I could retain some part of me which she couldn't touch, but I always tried not to cry or show emotion. However, this time, with danger so close, I couldn't take it anymore. 'Please, please, don't burn me, don't burn my hands.' She started laughing at me. 'Does little Donna not want her handies burned? Is little Donna scared? Well, maybe, just maybe, you should have thought about that before acting like such an evil little witch then,' she ended with a shout. I didn't care what she said – the poker was moving away from me. It had been so close to my hands that, even now, I can still feel the heat burning me. She stuck it back in the fire as I gasped with relief and scrambled away to my room. Maybe even Helen had boundaries. Everyone else would see if she burned my hands, so perhaps it was just an empty threat, I reasoned to myself.

I should have known better. Helen wouldn't give up such a good game when she had only just discovered it. Over the next days and weeks, I almost got used to that poker. Every time it seemed to come a little closer. Sometimes it grazed me. She held it so close to my face that I could feel the heat, even although it never touched me completely. I was scared to death that she was going to burn me. What would tip her over? 'I only do this because you're so bad,' she would say. I didn't want to be bad, I wanted to be good; but I didn't know what I was doing that was so terrible.

All around me, normal life went on. Helen was still shouting at me and calling me names, but the little slaps and pushes had now given way to out-and-out punches and kickings. I was being beaten regularly, for absolutely no reason at all. The flat on the left of ours belonged to Mr and Mrs Woods. They were absolutely lovely, and I would try to see them whenever I could. As time went on, my dreams of being rescued – of someone seeing how mean Helen was – focused on the Woods, but she was good at maintaining a pretence with them – I'm sure they only ever saw her as a young woman, baby on hip, with a heavy burden to carry.

I can't remember having anything that belonged to me, any personal possession. In my room there was a photograph of Frances, Simon and myself before we went into Barnardo's, and it gave the place the only bit of homeliness I could focus on. I was still waiting for them to come home, still sure that everything could be perfect once they arrived. Although Frances had a little smile on her face in the photograph, the three of us looked sad and confused. Helen would often ridicule us because of the image – with me it was 'look at the petted lip'. This was a favourite saying of hers – 'get that petted lip off your face!' or 'what's the petted lip for?' I never knew what she meant, but I did know it was something else to make her mad.

In terms of other family or household possessions, I have to filter it all through what was happening to me. We did have a television at one point, but I didn't get to watch it. I would generally be standing in a corner, or in the recess, or in the hall, when Helen's favourite programmes would start up. I knew what the telly was like when it was switched off – a big black screen in a wooden surround with Bakelite knobs – but what it spewed out impinged on me only as background to one of my punishments. *Z Cars*, *Dixon of Dock Green*, *Coronation Street* – they were all theme tunes I recognised, and vague voices I heard regularly, but there was no interaction for me.

It was the same with radio. Helen loved music – she called the radio and her Dansette her 'treasures'. Sunday afternoons she would cook food I was never allowed to eat, while the smells wafted towards me wherever I was being punished, and the sound of *Sing Something Simple* came from the radio, with the high-pitched tones of the performers singing their old-fashioned medleys. Helen played the Beatles, Andy Williams, Nancy and Frank Sinatra, Sandy Shaw. Just hearing a few bars of 'These Boots Are Made for Walking' can transport me back there, even now.

Music didn't soften Helen Ford. It may have provided a

soundtrack to my abuse and neglect, but it did little else. It wasn't long before I was constantly tense, always waiting for something to happen. I knew that most days I would be punished.

I'd be sent to stand in the damp recess for hours.

Punched.

Starved.

Slapped.

Stripped and made to wait in the freezing bathroom.

Screamed at as a witch.

Kicked.

Threatened.

Have a burning poker held to my face.

Told I was ugly.

And I learned to expect it all.

Chapter Five

༄

MY LITTLE LIFE

1964–1967

THAT WAS MY LIFE at Easter Road. That was what I was given instead of Haldane House. I was too little, too inexperienced to know that keeping things the same would never be enough for someone like Helen. She always needed to be the boss, to have me terrified, and I was getting too used to the punishments being meted out.

I was still young enough, still naïve enough, to think that things would get better. After a few weeks at Easter Road, the next big change in my life loomed large. I was going to school! For most children, the first day at primary school is a big deal. Weeks of preparation, of buying the uniform, getting a new pencil case and pencils, culminate in the day itself. Photographs are taken, and the child in question is generally left feeling rather special. That didn't happen for me. I knew that I was going to Leith Walk School, and I knew that it would be happening on the morning of Monday 24 August 1964, but that was where it all ended. There was no real excitement in the family, and even though Helen's real cruelties had not begun in earnest, the lack of occasion given to my first days in the big world was perhaps a warning.

When the day itself came, I was simply up and dressed as

normal, and taken along the road by Helen, with Gordon in his pram. I was excited – but I kept it as quiet as I could. I do remember her giving me a ticking off for skipping as we went along the street. I do remember that she pretty much shoved me through the gates and left me to fend for myself. Other children were there with parents or older siblings. They were trying to look brave, or crying, or casting their eyes around rather bewildered. I was just left to get on with it.

I had high hopes though. Maybe this was where my normal life would begin; maybe this was where I would become a little girl just like all the others. Not a Barnardo's kid. Not a stepchild. Just me.

It never happened.

I did try. I tried to learn, I tried to play, I tried to make friends. But I was to become labelled, marked by the cruelties and abuses which Helen would be dishing out to me in such force so soon. All around me, adults would be able to close their eyes to the physical marks – the fact that I was so small, so skinny, so hungry, so bruised – but children don't work like that. They knew there was something else about me. The smell. The look. The attitude. I was an outsider very quickly, and school didn't become the haven I had hoped for.

Teachers certainly didn't save me from the world that was going to suck me in, but they weren't the only ones. There were other people who should have been looking out for me – but Helen was too quick, too sly, too clever for them. It's incredible really. This barely educated woman, hardly out of childhood herself, would be able to run rings round the authorities for years. My father was rarely around, and she made sure that he most definitely wasn't there on any occasion when her words and the reality of the situation I was living in might tell different stories.

As a child who had been with Barnardo's for some time, there were obviously some rules and regulations in place. As I have already said, there were concerns about handing over my half-siblings to my own father, given that he had no biological link to them. Similarly, when I was taken from Haldane House and returned to the Edinburgh flat, I was part of a paper trail which would be punctuated with visits. Staff from the social work department and from Barnardo's would come to Easter Road at various times to check on my progress and that of Simon and Frances when they arrived. From what I can tell, letters would be sent to my home with a date and time of the proposed meeting – in effect, giving Helen a chance to clear the decks. She knew when my father would be out, or could make sure that he would be. In fact, there are notes from her in my Barnardo's file acknowledging the planned visit times and stating that, unfortunately, her husband would not be able to attend. Conveniently.

When Helen knew the Barnardo's staff were coming, there was always a summit meeting. She would make me stand in front of her and then the warnings would start.

'Do you want to go back to the home?'

No.

I didn't want to be a child without a family again. I just wanted the family I was in to be so much better, so much kinder.

'You'd better tell the truth when they come. Do you know what happens to little girls who tell lies?'

No.

But if I was living this hell despite being good, what on earth would happen to me if I deliberately went against Helen? She was turning night into day, black into white. I would be asked questions about how my life with her was – and I was being warned not to tell lies. What lies? I would be lying if I said I was happy. Lying if I said she was nice to me. Lying if I said I was loved and warm and satisfied and cared for. Is that what she meant?

'You know what to do, don't you? You know?'

No. No. No.

I didn't know what to do. How could I?

She answered her own question.

'Of course you bloody well do – but you're too stupid or pig-headed or difficult to help me out, aren't you? Well, let me tell you, madam, so there's no room for doubt. You don't speak unless you're spoken to. You don't tell them anything unless they ask.'

But that wasn't it, really, was it? If they asked if she hit me, could I say she did? If they asked if she didn't feed me, could I tell them how hungry I felt? If they asked if she never hugged me or told me I was pretty, could I say how bad it felt? I knew I couldn't.

'They ask if you are well looked after – you say "yes". They ask if you like being here – you say "yes". They ask if I'm good to you – you say "yes". I want them leaving here thinking you're living with a fucking saint – you hear me, Donna?'

It was all about appearances, all about what other people would think of Helen, and I had to collude with it all. I had to help her make a pretend Helen – ironically, the type of Helen I truly wanted as my stepmother, the type she was so far from being.

I don't remember how many visits there were from the social work department or Barnardo's, or from anyone else who may have had a professional interest in me, but I do know that they all took on the same form. On the day of a visit, I would be fed – and the feeling of the food, the knowledge that I wouldn't be hungry that day, made me so grateful that I always thought it was the start of things going well. Only later did I realise it was nothing more than a bribe. I would have my hair brushed and be put in clean clothes. Much more attention would be paid to Gordon, even though he wasn't the subject of the visit. Her golden child would be dressed up in his best clothes and paraded as a perfect specimen of what Helen, the good mother, could produce. Any faults would then be seen as mine – if she did so well with Gordon, it was inconceivable that I wouldn't be cared for.

I knew what to do – I knew to answer the questions as she wanted me to, and never to offer extra information. When my Dad came home, Helen would, of course, tell him that I had given her a 'showing up' and I would get walloped again. It's hard for me to comprehend how blind my father chose to be. Did he never ask any questions? Did he never have any suspicions? Did he never want to be involved?

૭

I was always thinking that things would be different once Frances and Simon arrived. In Haldane House, we hadn't been together all the time, but I knew they were there. Because I was still so little, they were my brother and sister to me; there was no talk of half-siblings or different fathers.

This lack of paternity for Simon and Frances has always bothered me. I suppose, to begin with, Don Ford might have had some notion of responsibility to my Mum's other children; perhaps he even thought she would be home soon and he would try to keep us all together for that day. I can only assume that, at some point, he realised this wasn't going to happen, and that looking after three tiny children and holding down a job – even with the help of the teenage Helen Gourlay – was more than he could manage. But why did he and Helen take all three of us back to Easter Road eventually? I had been there for eight months by myself, with things getting progressively worse, when Simon and Frances arrived 'home'. In later years, when I questioned why all of us were 'rescued' from Barnardo's, given what was waiting for us, I was told by one family member that the initial reason had been a practical one. The flat in Easter Road had been bought by Frances's father for Breda. I don't know what happened regarding ownership, but I do know that the imaginary continuing presence of Breda, my mother, continued to haunt Helen. She hated anything that reminded her of her predecessor, so the fact that we all lived in a flat which had been bought for Breda (even if, ultimately, for her daughter), a flat in which she had given birth to her three children, a flat in which she had loved my father, was anathema to Helen. Having me there was bad enough, but why put up with another two children who had no blood link to her – or, indeed, to her husband? I have been told that Helen wanted to move to a bigger house, a council one, and rent out the Easter Road property. By taking on even more children, she must have thought that being rehoused would be more likely. It seems strange now that the council would have allowed them to keep a privately-owned home while using up rented accommodation, but things must have been different in those days, and files from Barnardo's seem to confirm this. It seems that Helen wasn't a rescuing angel – she just saw us as a means to an end. We were potentially useful – with Frances, Simon and me in Easter Road, along with two adults and Gordon, things would be intolerably cramped and the council could come to our rescue.

It never happened. Helen was apparently told, after taking Frances and Simon in, that because they weren't my father's children, they couldn't be counted in our family total for rehousing. She had been thwarted and we would pay the price.

By the time Frances and Simon came back, most of my childhood fantasies about a perfect family life had been shattered. Given my own experiences, this time I knew there would be no party, no warm welcoming, no balloons around the door and cake on the table. In fact, as far as I can remember, the day they were brought back blended in with all the others. One minute they weren't there; the next they were.

I have a clear memory of seeing Frances again after such a while. She was so beautiful! My half-sister had the most gorgeous long, dark hair and I just wanted to stroke it, and dream of looking like her one day. To begin with, Simon and Frances were dragged around to see all of our relatives, just as I had been, and Helen was sure to take her fair share of the compliments wherever we visited. I would listen to all of these people, my flesh and blood, praise her to the heavens, saying she was an angel to take on this brood of kids who had no link to her, and I'd think of what she did to me. I wondered how and why adults could be so ignorant and let such bad things happen to children. Did they see nothing? Or did they know and not care?

Like me, Frances and Simon had a rude awakening – they quickly realised that Helen was not the kindly mother figure we all hoped for.

$\sim$

Frances's hair was one of the first things to go. Helen couldn't stand anything pretty or worthy of praise, so one day she sat my sister on a chair in the living room. She held Frances's hair up in one hand. 'Pleased with this, are you?' she asked. Frances already knew that there were never right answers where Helen was concerned. Silence was generally the best answer until you could gauge where she was going with her questions. 'Pleased with your lovely hair? Take after your Mum with it, do you? Everyone tell you how pretty you are, do they?' All the time, Helen was lifting Frances's hair up, twirling it round her hand, then letting it drop.

It was only after this had been going on for what seemed like ages that Helen pulled a pair of scissors out of her pocket. 'Vanity's a terrible thing, Frances – a terrible thing. Anyway – I'm sure it'll all grow back again.' She then chopped off all her beautiful hair. And made as bad a job of it as she could. It wasn't a haircut; it was a scalping. Frances sat there and cried and cried as her hair fell about her feet. There was no hiding from it any more – Helen was going to hate Frances and Simon just as she hated me.

Again, what was my father's role in all of this? He must have seen the evidence of Helen's hatred when he came home that night. He couldn't have failed to notice that Frances had been scalped. He and Helen were always fighting, always shouting, so perhaps they did argue about things like that – but, if they did, it was never enough to change things, to make him do anything.

Soon after Helen chopped off Frances's hair, she got us all together to tell us 'the rules'. We were all made to stand in the living room with our hands by our sides, like little soldiers. Helen rattled through a list that she was making up as she went along – don't speak unless you're spoken to; don't take anything at all without permission; don't talk to anyone without me saying you can; don't suck up to your Dad; don't expect me to be a mother to you. The list went on – most of it washing over me, as I knew that there was no rhyme or reason to Helen's 'rules', and that adhering to them all wouldn't save you in the slightest. But Simon and Frances – although terrified – still seemed to think that if they could only remember it all, and stick to it, then life might be bearable. They still had hope. I was running out.

Our stepmother dealt with my half-brother and sister in different ways. Frances was almost 10 when she came back, so Helen could make use of her. I suppose it was also more difficult to intimidate the eldest of us completely, although she did try with incidents such as the hair-scalping. More than anything, Helen found Frances quite handy. She would be sent on lots of errands – to the shops, to neighbours, to collect bits and bobs, or to take messages between Helen and her friends. Helen would use Frances to walk the baby and even cook the dinner.

On one occasion, I had been playing in the back green when I fell and hurt myself. Predictably, Helen showed no sympathy – her only response was to tell Frances that 'if she wanted', I could be taken to the 'sick kids hospital' to be checked over. It was a long bus journey, and I remember being so proud of my big sister as she found the hospital, spoke with the receptionist at accident and emergency, and then related my fall to the doctors. A few times, I remember staff asking where my Mum and Dad were, and telling Frances what a good girl she was. They must have found it odd that such a young child was in sole charge of another, but they stitched me up and we made our way back home again, alone.

~

Simon had a different strategy, imposed rather than adopted. While Frances made herself useful and I continued to be the little bastard who bore the brunt of the physical abuse, my half-brother became the centre of Helen's ridicule. From making fun of the way he looked, to playing practical jokes on him that weren't in the least bit funny, there was no end to the amusement she got from this skinny, insecure, nervous little boy. One day she called him through to the living room. 'Time to stop being so useless,' she informed him. 'At least your big sister can actually do some things if you get it through her thick head.' Simon stood there trembling. I could see that he was trying to remember the 'rules', trying to figure out what he should do.

'I want you to try and make yourself useful too,' said Helen. Simon nodded vehemently. 'Get yourself sorted, get your coat, and get yourself off down Easter Road. I'm not sure what shop you'll need to go into, so best try them all. Go into every one, every single shop mind you, Simon, and ask them for a left-handed screwdriver. Make sure everyone in the shop hears you, and don't take "no" for an answer. Don't you come back here until you've got me what I've asked for – a left-handed screwdriver. Do you hear me? You useless, *glaikit* boy? Do you hear me? Has it gone in?' Simon nodded again and set off on his humiliating journey. I can only imagine what happened next – the slight boy going into every shop each side of Easter Road and tremulously asking for something that didn't exist, something which was such a good joke to everyone else, but just another method of degradation for Helen to inflict on us.

Eventually Simon came back – empty-handed of course. He couldn't even bring himself to speak to Helen. 'Well, where is it, stupid?' she asked. 'Where's the screwdriver?' Simon just looked down. She got up and walked up to him, pushing her face down to his. 'Oh, Simon. That's just not good enough, is it? You didn't try hard enough, boy. You didn't do what I asked you to do. Do you know what you need to do now?' Simon was shaking. What did he need to do? Get her something to hit him with? Lie down so she could kick him? Bend over so she could beat him? 'Go back out again. Try Leith Walk. Every shop now, Simon, every shop.' The fact that Helen was offering him a non-violent option brought such relief that my big brother raced out of the house. Leith Walk ran parallel to Easter Road and was a huge shopping street with flats above all the outlets. You could buy anything on Leith Walk; it was – and still is – the heart of multicultural, 24-hour Edinburgh, and Simon probably had high hopes for his elusive left-handed screwdriver purchase. To walk the length of Leith Walk, both sides, and go into every shop would be quite a project even for an adult, but Simon set off on his mission.

When he returned hours later, empty-handed, he was weeping. He came into the house and shamefacedly went towards Helen. She said nothing this time – just launched into hitting him straight away, constantly telling him he was useless and a cissy. To this day, I think of all those shop-owners and customers probably having a good-natured giggle at the wee boy asking for a left-handed screwdriver, perhaps thinking he was on a childish dare, perhaps thinking he was winding up the shop staff, but no one knowing the hurt which was really behind his errand.

၃

Whatever the details of the homecoming of Frances and Simon, nothing much changed for me. I should have guessed really – although Helen didn't like an audience of adults when she laid into me, kids didn't matter. She was as happy to hit me and scream at me in front of Frances and Simon as she had been before their arrival. And a nine-year-old and seven-year-old couldn't do anything to save me, not that I ever saw any evidence of them trying to. When you live in fear, when you live with the constant terror that you can be belted and whacked and punched at any second – especially when you are five years old and your attacker is a grown woman – you think about yourself rather than others for most of the time. It was the same for Frances and Simon. At times, my half-sister and half-brother would be there while I was being beaten, and at times I would witness attacks on them. Sometimes, each of us would watch in horror; sometimes we'd turn our faces away; always we'd be grateful it wasn't us getting it. In the middle of it all, Gordon, who was now two, was watching and learning.

One day, when I was about six, Frances and Simon ran away together. I was either too scared to go, or never invited – I can't remember – but I do recall them being brought back home by the police. Helen acted terribly concerned and awfully relieved – but the door was barely closed on the helpful officers before all three of us were thrashed over the bath with a belt then made to scrub all the floors in the house. All the time Helen was screaming that we were never ever to call her 'Mum' as she wasn't our mother and never would be. I think that was just about sinking in by now.

༄

Another time, standing in my room, facing the wall after God knows how many hours, I heard Helen shout for me. She was in the living room, and I immediately walked through, still in my vest and knickers. There was no sign of Frances or Simon, although Gordon was sitting beside his mother on the floor. Helen stared at me. Her eyes never really showed any emotion (even when she was incredibly angry, she seemed to be somewhere else). It was as if she could just remove herself from where she was, from where I was, and get on with the job in hand, the pretend job for which she had created made-up rules. Maybe that's what abusers need to do – perhaps there is a part of them which needs to disassociate itself from what they are actually inflicting on a child. Or maybe it just becomes bread and water to them, and they couldn't actually care less any more. Something seemed different this time – there was a tone to her, a feeling about the whole thing, a lack of control even more frightening than usual that made the hairs on my forearms stand up on end.

I didn't know what to do.

Something was coming, I knew that. Something new. Something she had only just thought of. Should I cry? Should I beg her to stop whatever it was going to be? Should I laugh? Should I defy her? What would anger her more? What would mollify her? Even as an adult, I wouldn't know how to act with someone like that, so the very idea that a six-year-old might know how to cope is laughable. Despite this, all these strategies ran through my mind. And always, always, there was the hope that I could do something to turn this awful woman into someone – something – more human.

Her eyes remained cold, then a spark briefly came into them. 'Come here, Donna,' she said, stretching out her hand. 'Come here for a wee minute.' I had to take her hand, I had to go with her. The pull of some contact – no matter what would greet me at the end of it – was too much to resist. She took me – dragged me – along the lobby. We were going outside. Maybe she was going to knock on Mr and Mrs Woods' door. Maybe she was going to tell them what a bad girl I was and shame me in front of them. It looked like that was her plan as we continued out of the front door. But we walked past their flat and started to climb the stairs. Where were we going? She couldn't take me outside in my underwear, could she? Then people would know, people would know that she didn't act like a good Mummy, a nice Mummy.

But we weren't going outside.

We stopped at the door to the coal cellar.

She crouched down beside me. 'Look, Donna. Do you know what's in there?'

I nodded. It was the coal cellar and I told her so.

'Think you're smart, do you?' she snarled. 'It's not just a coal cellar, Donna. It's a place where bad girls go. It's a place for nasty, evil wee witches. Ugly little bastards who don't deserve good things or nice mummies get locked in coal cellars, Donna – and they never know if they'll get out again. Maybe nobody would know you were in there, Donna. Maybe nobody would ever remember to let you out again, Donna.'

I was shivering. Shaking. This was what she was going to threaten me with now, was it? Well, she'd won. She'd got me. I'd do anything, anything she could think of, anything she could make up, to avoid going in there.

She looked at me. 'Come on then, Donna. Let's go.' When we got back into the flat, I'd be brave enough to ask her – that was where we must be going now, and I would just come right out with it, I would come right out and ask her what I could do to avoid ever, ever, ever being put into that place.

'Come on,' she said again, and I realised that the hand holding mine wasn't taking me back downstairs to the flat. It wasn't taking me home. It was slowly dragging me towards the door of the coal cellar. She was taking me in there. This wasn't a threat. This wasn't a warning. This was real.

I was going in.

The wooden door creaked open as she turned the key in the

lock. I whimpered. I couldn't help it. Even though I knew it might anger her, I was so scared, the noise just slipped out of me. Just inside the door were a few wooden steps which took you down into a dark, dank, musty, dirty space. I tried to cling on to her hand but what chance did I have? She slipped hers away from me, shoved me down the steps – and smiled.

'Have a nice time, Donna. Have a nice time.'

The door was locked behind me as I waited for my eyes to get used to the dark. But they didn't. They couldn't. There wasn't a single chink of light for me to focus on. I was frightened, lonely, sad and sore (I was always sore), and now I was in a place where I might be left forever.

The utter terror and complete sense of loneliness was overwhelming – so many adults have an absolute fear of the dark, and yet here I was, a tiny, undernourished, unloved, beaten child being locked into a pitch-black, freezing place. I felt as if I could touch the blackness. I kept hearing the sound of the lock turning over and over again in my memory. What could I focus on? How could I get through this?

All I could do was think of the sunshine, think of being outside. I thought that if I concentrated enough, I might be able to make a picture in my head, and forget I was there. I told myself not to scream – she might be outside listening and that could make her even angrier. I knew I mustn't wet or soil myself – if I did, she would only rub my face in it when – if – I got out and scream at me for being disgusting. What was left for me to do? How could I pass the time not knowing if it would be minutes or hours? Or even, God forbid, days? The longer I thought about it, the more worked up I got – no one knew I was here! She could say I'd run away. She could leave me here forever – I could die in this hell hole.

I had to believe it would only be for a few seconds, even while my head and heart were screaming that she'd never let me off so lightly. I could cope. I'd have to cope. It was only darkness, wasn't it? There wasn't anyone in here. I wasn't being kicked or punched. I could get through this.

Then the noises started.

At first, I tried to tell myself I was imagining it. I hummed very quietly to myself, little bits of songs I'd heard on the radio. I couldn't sing loudly because of the fear that Helen would be outside the cellar door. But quiet humming wouldn't drown out what I could definitely hear. This wasn't in my mind, and it was getting louder, more frantic. Closer.

Scraping. Burrowing. The feel of wet noses against my bare legs. The touch of wet fur against my shins. I could feel sniffing and inquisitive bodies wondering who this intruder was. I was surrounded.

There was nothing to focus on except the scraping of what I now knew were dozens of rats beside me. They got more and more confident, and I had to deal not only with their presence and their scraping about, but also with the squealing which now filled the cellar. They must have picked up on the fact that I was weak and wasn't going to pose a threat so they started to reclaim their territory. The squeaking didn't seem to stop; their investigation of me didn't seem to stop. I was absolutely terrified as the sound filled my ears. Would they bite me? What would they do to me if I was there for days? For weeks? I could feel their fur against my legs, but eventually I had to sit down, even though I knew I was making it easier for them to crawl all over me. And they did. After a few moments, the scurrying around me changed to a clambering as they climbed on top of me, I felt them over every part of my body. I sat there, with my hands over my eyes, quietly sobbing, every inch of my body shaking as filth-ridden rats climbed across me in the pitch-blackness.

Suddenly, other things in my life seemed so much more bearable. The backhand slaps she gave me with hands covered in rings that scraped my face. The insults and screaming before the near-naked degradation in the bathroom. All of that, and more, was so much better than this.

Hours later, she came for me. The door opened silently. She didn't say a word, just waited for me to find my feet and climb out. I staggered back to the flat, where nothing was said by anyone. I fell into my room, knowing that there was something new, and even more horrific, in Helen's repertoire.

As I stood by the wall, freezing and in shock, I looked behind me as she closed the door.

'Witch,' she hissed. 'You fucking stink.'

৵

The days continued, into weeks and months. I spent my first Christmas with my new family in that hell hole, and it was as miserable as all the other birthdays and Christmases that would follow. No one could have survived the sort of terror I had been through in that house every day. Beatings and hatred marked my everyday life – there was always something, and some days the something was even worse than usual.

Looking back on it, I do wonder where my father was in all of it. Did he really see nothing? I was so thin, so covered in bruises and so terrified that, as a parent myself now, I find it laughable to think that a father wouldn't notice. Maybe he did see and didn't care. Or maybe he chose not to see. He certainly spent most of his time at work. When he came back, he was faced with Helen shouting at him about how unhappy she was, how little money she had, how he had to work harder, do more hours, get an extra job. Perhaps he just switched off. The only time she ever spoke to him about me was to complain. I was evil. I gave her funny looks. I was difficult. She would tell him he had 'no idea' what I was like. And she was right. He was absolutely clueless. How could a grown man not notice that Frances had been scalped? That Simon was terrified? That I was starved? My father does not escape from this story without guilt, and I will never know just how much he did collude with Helen in my misery.

He and Helen were obviously still maintaining some sort of relationship because when I was seven my next half-brother was born. This time, I was under no illusions. Gordon was four by this time, and Helen had turned him really nasty. I had no reason to suspect that Andrew, the new child, would be any different.

But things were about to change. Our family was getting bigger, but the announcement that we were going to move house came as a surprise – a very welcome one. We weren't moving far – only a few hundred yards really – to another part of the Easter Road area. Our new house was to be in Edina Place, and, to me, this represented the possibility of a new beginning. Perhaps the family life I had dreamed of when in Haldane House would magically appear once we left the increasing hell of our flat in Easter Road.

I was about eight years old when we moved, and all I knew was that the new house would have more space. With five children, this could only be good. I had spent the three years at Easter Road since my return from Barnardo's in a state of terror. From Helen's initial labelling of me as a 'bastard' and a 'little witch', I had lived through one horror after another. I had no life at all. Even at school, I couldn't relax. Helen had the time it took me to travel to and from school worked out to the nearest second. I was told when to leave the house in the morning, and she made sure I had no time to play or dawdle. She knew exactly how long it took me to get home again, and God save me if I was later than she deemed accurate. I couldn't breathe for a moment – I couldn't play skipping before the bell went, I couldn't play hopscotch on the way home. Everything revolved around my fear of my stepmother and what she would do to me if I was late. A part of me hoped against hope that the move to the new house would distract her and perhaps buy me some breathing space to do all the normal things which little girls should do. It wasn't asking for much – but it was never going to happen.

Helen was already honing her cruel skills on me, but I would soon find that in Edina Place, she would have even more freedom. It would become so much easier for her to imprison me without other people noticing at all. My new beginning would become nothing more than a fresh hell.

We did the move ourselves, roping in other family members, Dad's mates from the pub, and anyone else who was around that day. It would look funny now to see an entire family trailing their worldly goods from one side of the street to the other, but it wasn't so unusual in those days. The pram, which had already seen a lot of use, was now put into action as our removal 'van'. It would get piled up with as much as we could balance, string tied across the top, and wheeled over to the new place time after time. There was a non-stop procession that day from Easter Road to Edina Place, with people coming and going, helping out when they could. I can remember the day itself quite clearly and I knew that Helen would be fine as she had an audience to play to.

For me, the years at Easter Road had been focused on punishment, and wondering what I would have to endure each time she came near me. The physical and emotional abuse escalated relentlessly. Looking at the overall picture, it was an incredibly fraught situation. Nothing excuses what my stepmother did to me, even in those early years, but we were living in tiny quarters with two young babies and three children who had spent so long in a children's home. It would be hard for anyone. Add Helen's particular brand of evil to the mix and things were reaching breaking point.

And I was the one she wanted to break.

Chapter Six

৶

New Beginnings

1967

AS SOON AS I saw Edina Place, my heart soared. This, I felt, would be where things would change. The house seemed absolutely massive. Although it was a tenement with people living above us, we were a cut above – having the main door flat meant we didn't share stairs with anyone else. It was ours. I thought we were incredibly posh. This type of house was common in Edinburgh then, and remains so.

The layout of Edina Place is important when I think of what was to happen to me there. After entering the main door, there was a vestibule with a terrazzo floor. The tiles were absolutely beautiful, and in keeping with the rest of the place which was immaculate when we moved in. An old couple had been living there and had clearly taken enormous pride in their home. We would soon wreck all of that. After the vestibule, there was a glass door leading to a very long hall, on which my Dad eventually did some work.

On the left-hand side going up the hall was the first room, which became the bedroom of Helen and my Dad. It was a big room with all the original wood still visible and a fireplace which could still be lit. The size of the room alone was enough to impress me, but what struck me more were the beautiful glass panels in the front windows. They were stunning, covered with birds of all kinds. The panels could be taken out to clean, but the reality was that the easy access meant they were sold at the earliest opportunity. The bottom half of the windows were decorated in a sort of opaque fashion to give some privacy, and above all the windows, running around the room, were lovely cornices.

After that bedroom, going up the hall, was a cupboard my Dad used largely for storage. He had originally trained as a French polisher so he had lots of tools and was always pottering around, doing things – badly – at home. He rarely finished these jobs, lending a cumulative feeling of neglect to wherever we lived. Further on from that cupboard was the pantry. Once we got organised, that would house the cooker and electricity box, and other things that kept the place running.

These rooms were all innocuous. They were part of where I was now living, but they wouldn't really play much of a role in my life. However, some rooms haunt me still. At the very top of the hall, facing the front door, was the bathroom. To this day, I shudder when I think of it. Helen had already shown how fond she was of incorporating our previous bathroom into her punishment routine – with this one she would go even further to make every day a living nightmare.

To understand the layout, it's easier to go back to the front door as the bathroom takes the house to a natural midpoint. By coming up the hall again from the front door, the first room on the right would become the boys' bedroom – Simon, Gordon and Andrew would all sleep there. It was a very square room, but the most important feature for me was that in the left-hand corner there was a door leading to a boxroom – mine and Frances's bedroom. That boxroom was to become the centre of my world. It would originally have been the dressing room in Victorian times, I think, and it still had a certain charm when we first moved in. Some of my Dad's do-it-yourself projects impinged directly on the room where I would be a virtual prisoner. Soon after we moved in, he tried to lower the ceiling in the hall. I think this was to try and create some sort of space above in which he could keep all the paraphernalia he collected. The only effect I could see was that he had put in huge beams which never did get cut to size, and which came straight through into the boxroom.

Coming back out into the hall again, the next entry would be the main door to the boxroom, with another cupboard beside it. Further down the hall was the last door on the right – the living room. In that room, which again was a very square shape, was a recess that aligned with the hall cupboard. A wooden door in the recess also led to the boxroom, so both the living room and the boys' bedroom had, in theory, access to the room which I would ironically call 'mine'.

Apart from these rooms, there was one other place that became important. Outside Helen's bedroom was a cellar. Many a time my father would take me down there, as Helen would scream at him that I 'needed' a leathering.

I can take myself back to my room in an instant. It was long and narrow with a really high ceiling. My bed was pushed against the door that led into the boys' bedroom, and one of their beds was pushed against it on the other side. Initially the décor of the room was dated but in reasonable condition. However, Helen and my Dad always seemed to need to interfere with things, and it was wallpapered over with woodchip. I hated it – and do to this day. I spent so long in that room, staring at nothing but sharp little pieces of wood poking out from the paper. I detest all wall coverings really, because I had to obsess about them so much as a child. In the parts where they hadn't put the woodchip, there was paper embossed with roses, glazed and dusky pink. Soon after we moved in, Helen renewed her routine of sending me to stand for hours at a time, facing the wall. I'd trace my fingers round those roses, thousands and thousands of journeys. The floors offered no comfort. There were no carpets or rugs, just plain floorboards, not sanded or varnished. Just cold. Inhospitable like everything else.

Frances lived in that room with me when we first moved in – but not for long and I felt so lonely when she left. I can only think that because Frances was the eldest, she was the hardest for Helen to control. Once my two half-siblings came home from Barnardo's, Helen tried to keep them down, just as she did with me. They too felt the back of her hand; they too were slapped and punched. But while Simon cowered and found his own ways of dealing with things, Frances often answered back. It used to terrify me. I wanted to be brave like her, but I was so scared of what Helen would and could do that I generally tried to keep as quiet as possible – not to complain about punishments, to not say that things were unfair, not to cry when tears were all I could think of. Frances would shout back. She would scream and stamp her feet. And she would run away. I know that she had disappeared while we were living at Easter Road, and she and Simon had also gone together once, as I've mentioned before. However, in Edina Place, the running away became more and more frequent. I have no idea what was happening to Frances, what was going on in her life, and I can only hope she was not experiencing the same hell as me.

One day, Frances left my life and I never saw her again. She hadn't been with us at Edina Place for long, and her time there had been characterised by running off and police visits. Where she went, I never knew – all I'm left with are yet more questions.

Whatever the real story, the outcome was the same – Frances disappeared from Edina Place not long after we moved in, and I was left alone in the boxroom.

↪

Loneliness was one of the main markers of my time there – little was I to know that one day I would yearn for it: being alone would be infinitely preferable to the horrors I would face when subjected to the attentions of others. My memories of Edina Place don't really cover many communal events because it was so unusual for me to be involved in anything resembling family life. Helen would have to be in an exceptional mood before I would be allowed into the living room. I do remember the initial buoyancy of moving, as things were a bit more relaxed for a short while, but it soon settled back into the familiar, horrendous pattern.

School days were pretty much all the same. I sprang up as soon as I heard the house waking as I didn't want to give her any chance to come in and start on me. From the moment I woke, I'd feel sick. There may have been nothing in my stomach, but I'd still feel nausea creeping over me as I wondered what sort of mood Helen would be in. Would it be a lucky day when she would only hit me a couple of times about the ears or head before I left? Or would there be a threat? 'Just. You. Wait. Until. You. Get. Home.' Those words would ooze out of her. She'd almost whisper them to me and they would hang over my entire day. The thought that she would have been brewing her anger all of the hours I was at school sent me cold. Her words would haunt me and I knew she'd always think of something else to make things worse.

Even seemingly little acts twisted the knife still further.

'You won't need this,' she'd laugh, and take the broken light bulb from its socket in my room, never to be replaced in all the years she was there.

'And what would you need a door handle for? You're not going anywhere,' she'd cackle, removing the handle from my side of the door – my only independent means of getting out of the room.

Keeping me in my place. Control. Making sure I knew she was in charge. Always.

I don't have dates for these constant cruelties. I didn't have a diary. I didn't log it all. But I do know that the physical, mental and emotional abuse piled up from soon after we moved into Edina Place until the day she finally left.

Playing it back in my mind and talking about it as an adult, I can see my own past as flashes. I can picture scenes in my mind, and the recognition that this is my own history retains the power to shock and, indeed, to take me back there. The memories I have may be Easter Road, Edina Place, a school day, a weekend or a holiday, but there are unchanging elements – the cruelty, the baiting, the overriding need for control on Helen's part, which allowed her to do those things to a child without ever flinching.

Food played such a big part in it all. Even now as an adult, I pay the price of those early years of forced starvation and torture. I have no idea what size child I would have been, how big I might have grown, but I know that, to this day, I can't eat as other people do. When I make new relationships, potential friends probably think 'eating disorder' because I am thin, I have problems with food, and it's obvious to anyone who spends time in my company. Sometimes it's easier to let them think that way, because how else should I explain it? My stepmother starved me? She treated me worse than a dog? She fed me scraps at best, and I stole food wherever and whenever I could?

Food was a weapon for Helen, one of the many in her arsenal. It had started in Easter Road, but intensified in Edina Place. Most of the time, I'd either be standing still in my room, tracing wallpaper roses with my fingers, or in the bathroom standing equally still, cold, half-naked and terrified. I'd listen to the others having their tea. First of all, I'd smell the food cooking; then I'd hear the table being set. As the minutes dragged on, plates would be scraped, and the noises of normal family life would go on. The façade of normality – apart from the fact that one member was completely isolated. As the chairs were pushed back, I knew what was coming.

'You!' Helen would shout. 'Get through here, now!'

Embarrassed by the fact that I was in vest and knickers, shivering and pathetic, I'd go through to where she was. 'Well, then,' she'd goad, 'what should we do with you tonight? What do you think, Gordon? What does she deserve?' Helen would then go through the charade of discussing with Gordon what I was entitled to. She knew, he knew, I knew that I had done nothing to 'deserve' punishment. I had certainly done nothing to deserve being starved. But this was a ritual just like all the others. My rations would be decided.

'She's been rotten today, Mum,' Gordon would wheedle. 'I don't think she should get anything.' They'd laugh and giggle to themselves, then the bargaining would begin. Did I deserve full rations? Rarely. Half-rations? Quarter-rations? Whatever I was going to get, I was grateful. If half- or quarter-rations were determined, I'd be sent back to my room, and Gordon would come along some time later, kick the door open and throw my food in. It would usually fall on the floor, but I didn't care. Sometimes, he would spit in it for good measure. I still didn't care. Half-rations meant one slice of spam, four chips and maybe a teaspoon of tinned spaghetti. Quarter-rations barely marked the plate. But even if I was on no rations at all, I would be 'allowed' to do the dishes while the rest of the family went about their lives. I managed to get something out of this, because at least I would be a little warmer while I worked, and, if Helen wasn't being too vigilant, I could maybe steal a few scraps the others had left on their plates as I scraped them into the bin.

And that was my life. A room without a light in it. A door without a handle. A belly without food. Standing still for hours. No friends. No love. And a father conspicuous by his absence. I was never allowed out of my room unless expressly let out by her. I got no food unless it was given by her. She was my constant jailer and she would never let me forget that I was completely dependent on her. I tried to get out for food but I hardly knew where to start. She'd put a padlock on the pantry door, the cupboard opposite the living room. Yet, despite the dangers, I devised a system of getting in, even if I rarely had the confidence to use it. I was so desperate for food that I had stolen a knife from the living room, a brown-handled steak knife. With this, I could poke the old brass fitting and turn the handle, opening my door. Then, standing on a chair, I could unscrew the hasp and staple, letting myself in to the pantry. I'd take a few biscuits or some bread, or sometimes just some dry cornflakes. I'd stash them on me, usually down my pants. Then I'd put everything back in place and get back to my bed where I'd devour whatever I'd pinched, under the blankets, as quietly as possible, my heart thumping in my chest. Despite the fear, I really felt I'd won at times like that. I'd beaten Helen at her own game – even if only for a few scraps that barely touched the hole of hunger at the centre of me.

॥

If I wasn't in my room, hungry or sore, I'd be at school. That should have been a release for me, a relief, but it wasn't really. I was still an outsider. I didn't really have friends, for lots of reasons. I wouldn't be allowed to go back to anyone's house to play. I certainly wouldn't be given permission for another child to come back to our house.

But, more than that, I was excluded because of what Helen had turned me into. I stank. I constantly smelled of pee. When I stood in the bathroom for hours on end, I wasn't allowed to use the toilet. If I needed to go, I had to wet myself. I wasn't allowed to change my underwear after that. Helen took great delight in rubbing my face into my stinking pants, making sure that she held me tight and close into the stench until I was heaving. Then I had to put them back on again. The knickers which were rank with stale urine had to be worn the next day as a mark of shame. Sometimes, when I felt brave, I would sneak them off in the middle of the night, turn the tap on as little as I was able and try to get the stench out. I'd leave them to dry overnight and hope for the best. It never worked. I was dirty and I smelled. Children prey on the weaknesses of their peers. I was the girl who smelled of pee. Others would hold their noses when I went past or complain if the teacher made me sit beside them. How were they to know? Teachers presumably thought I wet myself deliberately or that it was something of which Helen despaired – they didn't know that she inflicted it on me, and they never seemed to care.

On non-school days I'd be at home, usually in the bathroom on a punishment for breaking an imaginary rule. Sometimes I'd be called through to the living room after hours had passed, but only to do chores – usually the ironing, or perhaps to collect washing that I had to lug back to my bathroom prison and trample in the bath until my legs ached. Everything that wasn't punishment was based around cleaning. I'd be told to scrub floors with a nailbrush, scour windows until my hands were red raw, do the washing in cold water in the middle of winter in my vest and knickers – and I was so desperate to get out of the bathroom that it seemed like a liberation.

As soon as we moved to Edina Place, it became clear that Helen was going to use the bathroom for punishment just as much as she had in Easter Road. She was obsessed with that room and all that went on in it. I've obviously wondered, as an adult, what Helen was put through as a child herself to turn her into the monster who ruined my own childhood. In that one room, there must be a clue. Whatever was done to her, whatever abuses she must have suffered, must surely have taken place in a room where she, in turn, thought it necessary to inflict degradation upon me. I can remember just standing there for hours on end with my hands by my side. Those old houses were so cold, so unforgiving. Even when you were happy and just living a normal life, it was a case of running in and out of the freezing room as quickly as possible to 'do your business'. But I would be there for a lot longer – and I swear she'd forget I was even there.

As I've said, the irony was that I wasn't even allowed to go to the toilet while I was trapped in there. Sometimes I would plead, shouting out that I really really needed to go and that I'd do anything if I could use the loo. I soon learned that this would annoy Helen even more, and that if I ever asked, I had absolutely no chance. I soon gave up. The humiliation, the next day stink, all became second nature. If I moved, she'd scream that she could hear me and that I'd 'get it'. I believed she probably could hear me, because I could certainly hear everything from her part of the house. The sound of the television programmes continued, the background noise to my life, but I never saw any of them. Now, when the constant stream of reminiscence shows fills the weekend schedules, I see clips of programmes that are so familiar to my peers, but to me are the soundtrack of my mortification at the hands of my stepmother.

I thought I had it bad in Easter Road, but Helen's hatred of me really came out in Edina Place. In the bathroom, she would push my face against the mirror. 'Look at you,' she'd hiss. 'Look at your ugly, ugly face. You're such a little witch, Donna. Such an ugly little witch, just like your mother. I don't know how you can bear for anyone to ever look at you. You must turn their stomachs. That must be why you're so useless and so evil and so rotten. It's all because of this ugliness. It shows in your face and it comes out in everything you do.'

I believed her. I couldn't look in the mirror when she shoved my face into it because I was scared of what I'd see. If you are so ugly that you can't be loved by someone who everyone tells you is good and kind, then why would you want to look at that reflection? I was skinny Donna, the starved little girl. I was smelly Donna, the child who pissed her own pants and whom no one would sit next to. I was bad Donna, the child rescued from an orphanage but so naughty that she didn't deserve any kindness. And I was ugly, ugly, ugly Donna, the witch-girl so hideous that she couldn't even look at her own image for fear of what it might show.

I couldn't look in a mirror for many years after Helen left my life. And I didn't even look at the photographs of me as a little girl until very recently. When I finally did open my eyes and face up to what was in those pictures, I was shocked. Shocked by what I really was. Normal. Appealing. *Pretty*.

Helen took all of that from me.

Edina Place wouldn't be a new beginning – it would be nothing less than a new horror.

Chapter Seven

ॐ

AUNTIE NELLIE

1965–1967

ELIZABETH EWART CHANGED ME. To the rest of the world, this
formidable retired headmistress who lived in Paties Road in
Edinburgh's upmarket Colinton area was probably a bit of a
cliché. Unmarried, Auntie Nellie was very particular in her ways
and manners, and always so certain of what was 'the right thing'.
I had known her at both my homes – Easter Road and Edina
Place – but as I got older, I started to notice just how much she
meant to me, and this coincided more with my life at Edina Place.

To me, Auntie Nellie was my only hope. She was my Dad's
auntie really – his mother's sister – so she was, in effect, my great-
aunt. Names didn't matter – what did mean something was the
fact that Nellie took a shine to me from the word go. No matter
what was to happen to me, what was going to be done to me,
it was Auntie Nellie who was the biggest influence on my life. It
was Auntie Nellie who made me what I am, and it was Auntie
Nellie who has always made me so certain that good does
triumph.

Her house was a pristine 1930s bungalow, a million miles
away from the life I knew. It felt so rich and comfy; the entire
house was suffused with warmth and full of lovely old
furnishings. There was a grandfather clock ticking in the hall, a

barometer on the wall, a Bakelite telephone from the 1930s and shining brass irons in the fireplace. There was old mahogany furniture everywhere, tables that gleamed, and overstuffed armchairs with lace antimacassars draped over the back and on the armrests.

Auntie Nellie's bedroom was opulent and sumptuous. There was a huge wooden bed covered with an embroidered satin throw and matching eiderdown. On her three-mirrored mahogany dressing table was an array of magical, wonderful items – even though I didn't dare touch them, I still appreciated their existence. On top of an embroidered lace doily was a silver brush, mirror and comb set. Beside them sat a jewellery box surrounded by ornaments. In the box, treasures lay in miniature drawers – lace hankies, leather gloves, silk scarves. Nellie's bedroom smelled of lavender. Everywhere was gentle and in complete contrast to my hard, harsh world – soft carpets, soft cushions, soft throws!

There was a pantry full to the brim of jars of home-made jams and chutneys. Food that was just there, there for the taking – that, to me, was a miracle in itself. Beside the food were stacks of chinaware, all so dainty, so perfect.

It's hard to describe what that house meant to me – it was a refuge, a fantasy of what other homes could be like. It was story-book stuff compared to where we were living. Auntie Nellie even had her own headed notepaper, the epitome of class! Sometimes, I found it hard to believe she was actually part of our family – but I clung to it. If she was a relation, and if she loved me as much as she seemed to, then maybe there was some hope for me. Maybe things wouldn't stay as bad for ever as long as Auntie Nellie was there.

Even now, years later, I find it difficult to talk of her simply because she meant so much to me. She was a wealth of wisdom and knowledge, and was wholly instrumental in switching me on to reading, to books, and to the other world I could create in my mind. Her house was a dreamlike palace to the child I was, but she gave me much more than that. She gave me my imagination. I was allowed to meet up with Auntie Nellie about once a month – presumably, the joy of getting rid of me meant more to Helen than the pleasure she got from denying me everything else – and I lived for those days. I could hardly believe that anyone would take a special interest in me. Helen was already drumming it into me that I was ugly, that I was a little witch, that I was an unwanted bastard child. Auntie Nellie's attentions seemed so tenuous as a result – surely she would find out about me? Surely she would see what Helen saw any minute and everything would be taken away?

~

On the days when Auntie Nellie was due to collect me, I was full of apprehension. Would she turn up? Would it be as wonderful as before? The day itself didn't start off any differently in terms of Helen's treatment of me. 'Get up, you little bastard!' she shouted from the living room. I already had on the best clothes I could find and I was waiting, just sitting and waiting.

Suddenly, the doorbell rang. It was Auntie Nellie! I heard mumblings between her and Helen, but didn't dare come out until I was called for. As soon as we both stepped out into Leith, our adventure began.

Auntie Nellie was very posh in my eyes – even her clothes could tell you that. She was a typical 'Edinburgh lady' of that time, generally dressed in a lambswool twinset and tweed skirt. She wore black 'ladies' brogues, which were always polished to a high shine. One day she informed me that the coat I loved her wearing was a 'camel coat'. I thought this was the height of poshness – it was years before I realised it was made from wool that gave the appearance of camel hair rather than made from a few camels themselves! Auntie Nellie would never be seen without a hat when she went out, and I can remember her handbag as if it were on the table in front of me now – black patent with a gold clasp, hooked over her left arm. Her left hand was gloved and in it she held the glove of her right hand, whilst in the ungloved right hand would be a little purse which matched the main handbag. When it was really cold, Nellie would wear a real fur coat, not a mangy moth-eaten one but one that felt as soft as silk. Although she could be stern and pedantic in a school-marm sort of way, my Auntie Nellie was round, soft and warm.

'Today, Donna,' she said, squeezing my hand in hers, 'we will be taking high tea. It is very important that you know how to conduct yourself amongst people. It is vital that you realise the importance of good manners and etiquette. Today, my dear, we begin.'

Auntie Nellie and I jumped on a number one bus and began our journey up Easter Road. Behind us, we left the shabby shops and grubby tenements where I spent my days. The bus stank of fag smoke and old men, but I couldn't care less – my dignified, wonderful Auntie Nellie was beside me in her perfect clothes, with her perfect style, and we were getting away from it all. The bus took us past the Palace of Holyroodhouse and up the High Street. At the very top of the Royal Mile, we alighted and walked down the Mound with Edinburgh glittering all around us.

'This, my dear, is your city,' Auntie Nellie told me. 'You are part of it, and it is part of you. Never forget that you have a responsibility to yourself to be all you can – look around you and be inspired. Look around you at this city of wonder and history. These streets have been walked upon by royalty. Mary Queen of Scots put her feet on these same cobbles as you and I. Dignitaries and important people from all over the world have come to this magnificent place for centuries to be motivated, to become enthused by all that we have. Don't forget that – it's all there for you, Donna.'

As I looked around at Edinburgh Castle beside me, at the art galleries laid out before me, at Princes Street Gardens shining in the sunshine, I could believe what Auntie Nellie was telling me. I wasn't a little witch when I was away from Helen. I could just be a normal little girl, out with a loving relative, who truly could have the world at her feet.

Auntie Nellie was a perfect source of stories I never tired of hearing. Edinburgh has an amazingly rich literary heritage, and is also a city in which the tradition of oral storytelling was passed down to children of my generation. When Nellie picked me up from our house and we travelled up to Princes Street, I felt as if I was going back in time. The backdrop to our walks and talks was the castle, the crags and closes surrounding the city, and the famous stores which attracted tourists from around the globe. For me, Princes Street was the heart of it all. Although things were beginning to change, by the time I was taken out on our trips, Nellie could bring it all back. There were parts of the stories I could still relate to – the Scott monument towered over the scenery for me as it had for Nellie as a girl. The castle remained imposing. The 'Disgrace of Edinburgh' at the far East End continued to be a powerful symbol of how people in power could get things wrong.

But there were also details that I could only imagine. Auntie Nellie loved to tell me of the days when trams were the major traffic feature in the city centre. There had been tramlines on both sides of the street, with a constant stream of vehicles going up and down, and white-gloved traffic policemen waving their matching white-banded arms about. By the end of the 1950s, this system had changed and Princes Street was becoming more as we know it today, even although the tramlines lasted longer than the trams themselves. When Nellie and I walked along in our own little world, I often closed my eyes and imagined I was back in those days, which seemed so much safer and more comforting in the distance. I adored it when she told me of the shops and stores of her youth. The actual layout of Edinburgh city centre has changed little, but where once there were independent retailers and shopping experiences the envy of any city in the world, there are now tacky burger outlets, sex shops and fly-by-night pound stores. She would tell me stories of the East End of Princes Street where just past Jenners had been R.G. Lawrie's and the Old Waverley Hotel, a glove shop and a cigar retailer. The Scottish Omnibus Company now had premises there, where tourists and locals alike would buy tickets to explore the new layout of the city.

As we reached the bottom of the Mound, our destination appeared before us. The grand old lady of the world-famous Princes Street shopping parade would receive the distinguished company of two fine ladies today – Auntie Nellie and I were bound for Jenners, the department store which symbolises the capital and attracts the great and the good whenever they decide a trip to Edinburgh is on the cards. 'High tea at Jenners, dear,' whispered Auntie Nellie. 'What could be finer?'

Jenners' high teas were indeed a special treat. The store possessed a proper tea room with starched white tablecloths, upon which lay the most exquisite china and gleaming cutlery. Waitresses hovered, wearing black dresses covered with immaculate white aprons. There was a background warbling chitter-chatter from the 'discriminating' Edinburgh ladies, whose best hats and coats were always brought out for this occasion. Auntie Nellie was going to treat me – but it was also a learning experience. I would be told about all of the buildings we had passed and which surrounded us – the history of Princes Street, Edinburgh Castle and the Scott monument. Nellie would talk about how 'fine' the shops were in her day, and I listened to the list of names which were fast disappearing. Binns and Patrick Thomsons became memories passed down from Nellie to me, growing in stature as they were given the gloss of her retelling.

'Now, my dear,' she said, bringing me back to the present-day wonders of the Jenners' high tea. 'What will we have?' There was little point in asking me – I wouldn't have known where to start, and I certainly didn't think I had any right to ask for anything. But Auntie Nellie knew exactly what to do. Before my eyes appeared the most wonderful vision. A waitress stood at the side of our table with the china and chrome cake stand just for us. 'What do you think of this, my dear? Is there anything you like?' asked Auntie Nellie. Was there anything I liked? I didn't know where to start! At the bottom of the stand was an assortment of dainty sandwiches, all with the crusts cut off. Next, on the middle plate, stood Paris buns and scones of all description. On the top were the most beautifully coloured and decorated French fancies. I immediately decided to lunge for these gorgeous confections. Just as I went to make my move, a reserved voice broke into my reverie. 'My dear,' she intoned, 'whether in life or a cake-stand, one must always – always – start at the bottom and work one's way to the top.' The cakes were calling out to me, but I loved Auntie Nellie's ways so much that I was happy to take her advice – after all, an unlimited number of sandwiches was an indescribable treat for me too.

After our high tea, shopping was on the cards. Auntie Nellie often bought clothes for me on our monthly trips, but it was hard to keep them. Everything good I had always disappeared – I don't know whether Helen sold them or gave them away but, for a few hours at least (sometimes longer if my Dad saw them), I had lovely, warm, new, fresh clothes. Marks & Spencer would be our first stop, where Auntie Nellie would select woollen kilts and jerseys – warm, smart and very sensible. Next, she might buy me TUF shoes, which were an absolute delight as they had a compass in the sole – it was so unusual for me to have anything frivolous that even something as basic as a compass gave me enormous pleasure.

The entire day was a joy, but it was also an education. The ex-headmistress in Auntie Nellie never stopped, never went off duty. She taught me all about table manners, about how important it was to talk 'properly', the need for proper pronunciation and the evil of 'slang'. As we walked along Princes Street, bellies full of cake and arms full of shopping, I learned with every step. 'Just remember one thing, Donna,' she said. 'It doesn't matter what you do in life – just make sure you do it well. It is important to do unto others as you would have done unto you.'

Did Auntie Nellie suspect anything? At the time, I was so scared of her finding out that I was evil, that I had inherited badness from Breda, that I couldn't even have considered telling her what Helen was already making me go through. She would surely blame me, or perhaps warn me not to name-call or tell tales. How could I sully what I had with Nellie by verbalising the horrors of Edina Place? When I look back on it, I find it hard to believe that this intelligent woman wouldn't have suspected something. But, why then, didn't she take me away? Perhaps Auntie Nellie chose to remove me at specified times, to do what she could on our days out, because she recognised the power of Helen. Maybe she didn't want to engage in an all-out battle with her for fear of being excluded from my life for ever, for I am in no doubt that Nellie did love me.

At times, I struggled to understand the meaning of Auntie Nellie's words, but the sense of it all went into my very bones and now, as an adult, I can recall it perfectly. She gave me my love of reading, my love of travel, and she made me realise that I could be loved. But I do wish she had saved me.

Our trip over, it was time to head back to Auntie Nellie's house in Colinton. On the bus, she told me of her trips to Canada, of the great lakes and snow-covered mountains. It was all so far from my 'real' life and yet I so desperately needed to hear it. 'Settle yourself down there, dear,' she said as soon as we got in. I went over to her big, stuffed armchair by the open fire and prepared for an afternoon of watching BBC programmes. Auntie Nellie set the table, placing cutlery and china carefully over a huge lace tablecloth. As she taught me table manners, the cuckoo clock on the wall made its comforting noise. A man appeared on the left if there was rain, and a woman on the right if there was sunshine. It didn't matter to me – rain or sun, Auntie Nellie's was a haven.

These visits with Auntie Nellie started when I was about five years old. Forty years later, they are still engraved on my mind and my heart. I wanted them to go on for ever, but I should have known better. That wonderful woman was the centre of my world for those years. She was my one ray of light, my only hope. She treated me as a child, and as a human being. She was everything to me. Of course Helen couldn't stand that. Of course Helen had to stop it. But the cruelty and unfairness of what was to come still makes my heart feel as if it is breaking, even to this day.

Chapter Eight

୬

GORDON'S REVENGE

1967

I HAD NEVER HAD TO share Auntie Nellie with anyone – she hadn't shown any interest in Simon or Frances, who weren't related to her, so I got her all to myself.

Until one day.

It was time for my monthly trip to Auntie Nellie's, and I was eight years old. I was almost ready to believe that these days out with Nellie were real, that they weren't going to be snatched away, when Helen snapped: 'You. Take Gordon with you today when you go to see that old cow.'

Gordon was five by now. I didn't have much to do with Andrew, who was almost two by this time, because I had learned my lesson. I had invested some hope in Gordon when he was a baby – I wasn't going to make the same mistake twice. When I had first arrived at my new life with Helen and my Dad, the existence of Gordon had given me some hope. I had watched how my stepmother was with her first baby when she visited me in Barnardo's. She was warm and loving. She cuddled him and kissed him, and I always hoped that she would be like that with me. As time went on, and she started to make her hatred of me all too apparent, I was confused. She didn't hate all children, so why me? And I knew she had turned Gordon bad. I saw what he got up to – the stealing and swearing, the backchat and the naughtiness. He rarely got punished, and yet I was always being beaten, always sore. Why were things so different? Of course, Helen's constant reiteration that she wasn't my Mummy, and I was never to think of her as such or call her by that name, made it clear that blood – not circumstance – mattered. However, it still made me ache. Over and over again, it was made clear that Gordon was her flesh and blood, and he was the product of a 'proper' marriage. Even allowing for that, however, I thought I must be incredibly unlovable if she could hate me so much when she was obviously able to show love to another child.

When Gordon was little, I remember she would dandle him on her knee, singing nursery rhymes and basically just enjoying him. She had that capacity to love a child – with me, she chose the other route. I can hear her voice to this day – she would sing to him about 'Fatty Malatty, King of the Jews, sold his wife for a pair of shoes.' I was never dandled on her knee, I never had songs sung to me, and yet Gordon did not blossom with all this adoration – she turned him into a right little shit. Ironically, while I was the one given the names and labels, Helen's evil had managed to twist him into a child who really did seem like the Devil incarnate – at least to me.

During those early days in Easter Road, Gordon was a central part of what I see as the whole 'scene'. I would watch him with his mother and absolutely ache for some of what he got. The love and attention were tangible, but I was always excluded. In those first months, I was sometimes given a 'treat' of being allowed to play with Gordon, and I also learned that if I spoke about him, asked questions about him, showed an interest in him, then Helen would talk back. She just couldn't resist.

'Why is Gordon called Gordon?' I asked her one day.

If I'd asked such a basic, normal question about anything else, I would have got cold silence, but with Gordon on the agenda, Helen was soon in full flow. 'He's a very special boy,' she would tell me, 'and he needed a very special name. He's called Gordon after his Dad's eldest brother.' (No mention was made of the fact that this was also *my* Dad, and that Gordon's uncle was also *my* uncle.) 'He's called Andrew after my brother, and Chalmers because that's his Granny Ford's maiden name.' (Again, *my* Granny, *my* Granny.) 'Then, of course, he's called Ford, because that's the name of his Mummy and Daddy.' (*My* name, *my* name too.) At weekends, there would be a steady stream of visitors all there with one purpose – to fuss over Gordon Andrew Chalmers Ford.

Even by drawing attention to Gordon and asking questions about him, I couldn't manage to deflect Helen's hatred of me for very long. The first day she hit me is clearer than a lot of the things that followed, and Gordon's presence is so very clear in the middle of it all. I had said the word 'bloody' and that changed everything. I said it almost under my breath. I didn't say it to Helen. No matter that I was a child barely out of toddlerhood who had repeated a word she had heard a million times before. To make things even more laughable, I was only telling her that precious Gordon was a bit bloody where he had hurt himself while playing.

And I got smashed across the face for it.

The floodgates had opened.

～

Over the next year, I learned a lot of things. I learned that I was not important. I learned that I could be hit at will. I learned that she would never be a 'mother' to me. And I learned, time after time, that Gordon was special.

'Look at him!' she would scream at me. 'He is so, so special. And you're nothing. Nothing! Do you know why he's special? Do you? Do you know why Gordon is so special and you're not?' Sometimes I'd shake my head, sometimes I'd squeak 'no', but I could never guess the response she wanted. What she would be after one day would be enough to get me a slap the next. One thing never changed – her justification for the 'specialness' of Gordon. 'Gordon was born PROPERLY!' she'd screech. 'He was made in a proper, loving relationship with a proper Mum and Dad who are married. Not like YOU, you little BASTARD. You are a bastard child and you will always be a bastard child.'

It never altered. Gordon was perfect. He was an angel. He was loved and cared for and I wasn't. All because I had been born wrong. The fact that none of it – the lack of a marriage licence, my absent mother – was my fault, couldn't have mattered less to Helen. Her words were stuck in a groove and she never deviated from them.

Gordon was three years younger than me – and he was quick. He learned at the feet of a master and soon got the upper hand over the pathetic, trembling child I was becoming. His forte was telling tales – or 'clipping' – and nothing gave the special boy more pleasure than making up stories to relay to his mother. She'd love him even more when he could take her tales about what the bastard child had been up to – truth rarely came into it.

By the time we moved to Edina Place, Gordon was a full-blown bully. He took great delight in physically attacking me – punching, nipping, kicking and hair-pulling were all daily rituals. He'd also moved on to stealing things, knowing that I would be blamed. Gordon would frequently come into the bathroom when I was on my punishment (usually standing semi-naked, always freezing). He'd smirk and laugh at me, but I would always end up being blamed for that too if he was caught. I couldn't say anything – it was useless to even try. I was powerless to say anything to, or about, this golden boy of Helen's because I knew I'd end up even worse off. He could do no wrong.

Gordon was much bigger than me, even though he was younger. He glowed with health next to me – my scrawny, terrified little self couldn't compete with the golden boy and his regular meals, lack of beatings, and a mother who doted on him. They say children learn what they live – that didn't apply just to me but to Gordon as well. He watched his mother whack me every day, hit my head against walls, starve me, torture me, lavish me with nothing but neglect and abuse. And he learnt to do exactly the same. He could bully me into doing virtually anything he wanted. He'd get me to steal tanners or shillings from Helen's purse, which I would then have to hand straight over to him, or he would tell me I had to pinch some biscuits or crisps from the scullery. I did these things – things I didn't dare do for myself – because I was so petrified of this child that Helen clearly adored. If I didn't do what he said, he'd tell his mother some story and I would be beaten anyway. It was easier to risk doing what Gordon demanded in the hope that Helen wouldn't find out and I would at least avoid his wrath temporarily.

When Gordon started at the same primary school as me, any respite I had stopped. He was everywhere now. I used to love going to school, even though I was hungry and in tattered clothes, even though I had such a strict timetable to get home which was almost measured out in seconds. When Gordon followed, even that little bit of enjoyment was taken away from me. I had to look after him in the playground as, ironically, Helen was afraid he might be bullied. I had to take him to school and bring him home again, always knowing that he could see me at any point of the school day – that there were always eyes watching me.

I was already having to spend more time with him than I wanted, but the thought of him imposing on my time with Auntie Nellie was unbearable. I had to summon up the courage to plead with Helen, to beg her to allow me to keep this one thing for myself. 'Please,' I began to stammer, 'please, does Gordon have to … I mean, is it okay if he doesn't … maybe Auntie Nellie wouldn't want …' I couldn't even get the words out.

Helen's face came closer and closer to me. I tried to see if she had anything in her hand, because if she did, it would surely hit my face soon. But, instead of belting me, she laughed. 'Why do you want to keep that old bat to yourself?' she asked. 'If she's that great, why shouldn't Gordon get to go along? Get to stuff himself with cake like you, you greedy little bitch? Get things bought for him by some daft old mare with more money than sense?' At the mention of money, it suddenly became clearer. Of course, Helen would never pass up the chance of getting time to herself, especially if it made my day more miserable, but she had also been arguing more and more with my Dad about finances. I would hear them any time he was home, her screeching that we were always ready for the poorhouse, him saying he couldn't work any more than he already did. Helen was well aware that Auntie Nellie had no children of her own, and that she wasn't short of money, so her main concern was Nellie's legacy. On top of this, I had overheard a conversation one day between my Dad's aunt and my stepmother in which Nellie told Helen she had high hopes for me, and that she would do all she could to make sure I excelled academically. In Helen's eyes, that just wouldn't do – Auntie Nellie buying me clothes was one thing; taking me out for the day once a month could even be tolerated but the thought that I, not precious Gordon, might be getting long-term attention was just not an option.

So, Gordon started coming along on the visits. I should have known it wouldn't take long for him to wreck it all, but I was still naïve enough to think it couldn't get quite as bad as it did.

೩

I hated taking him to Auntie Nellie's. I didn't want him there, soiling what we had together. Gordon brought the stench of Edina Place with him and he reminded me of Helen every time I looked at his ugly face. When he slumped into one of Auntie Nellie's armchairs or messed up her ornament collection or guzzled his tea, I despised him so much for taking the one thing I had in my life. One Sunday while we were at Auntie Nellie's, Gordon motioned over to me while she was in another room. 'Have you seen this?' he whispered conspiratorially. I looked over at him from my chair. 'I'm not interested.' His eyes only ever sparkled when he was up to something – and they were like diamonds now. 'You don't even know what it is! How do you know you're not interested?' I knew that I was running quite a risk as Gordon's anger was like that of his mother – quick, unprovoked and generally aimed at me. 'Get over here, Donna,' he snarled. 'Come and see what Auntie Nellie has for us.' I didn't want him nosing about in Nellie's things. He was over at the sideboard where she kept all her china and crystal, her headed notepaper, and lots of other precious things which made her my own. I should have known Gordon wasn't interested in any of that. He'd found a purse full of change – that was all that had grabbed his attention. 'Take it, Donna. Take it.' He jangled the purse in front of me, rattling the coins inside. This was different. This wasn't like stealing from Helen, whom I hated, to give to her son, whom I also hated. This would be taking from a woman who had only ever given to me. Nellie had given me her love, her attention, her mind – all of which were more important than the money she had lavished on our high teas and my school clothes.

I tried to tell Gordon I just couldn't, but the look in his eyes made me realise it was useless. He may only have been a child, he may only have been five years old, but he had learnt so much from Helen. Some people question what children are capable of, what they can do – but over the years I've come to believe that those who are brought up as Gordon was can be incredibly manipulative and clever as children when it suits their ends, or the ends of those they are linked with. Helen pushed him to be what she wanted, her firstborn had to live up to her expectations – give a child the ammunition for what you want them to do and they can flourish. And that is what this boy did. I remember it as if it was yesterday.

'Take the stupid purse and go into the stupid old woman's toilet,' he hissed. 'Take the stupid money out of the stupid purse and throw it out of the window into the garden. When we get home, you give me the money. All of it. And you do it now, Donna, you do it now.'

I was eight years old. I was so scared and numb, and anticipating such bad things, that I did it. I turned my back on all the good things Auntie Nellie had done for me and did exactly as Gordon said. My heart was sinking from the moment I touched the purse. Giving the money to Gordon didn't take away the guilt. I knew it was the end. I had betrayed Auntie Nellie. I had ruined things again.

A few days later, Helen called me through to the living room. She could hardly contain her delight. 'Well, you dim-witted, evil little cow,' she began. 'What nasty things have you been up to now?' As she started on me, she waved a letter in front of my eyes. 'Auntie Nellie has been telling me all about her perfect little Donna. Donna with the high hopes and big dreams. Donna with it all ahead of her.' Helen read from the letter. We were no longer welcome at Auntie Nellie's house – and, according to the words my stepmother read, my great-aunt was heartbroken.

Helen was torn between the glee she felt at having finally split us up and the opportunity she was now presented with to beat the living daylights out of me. Before I had even entered the room, Gordon had easily convinced his mother that the theft had nothing to do with him.

'Get into the bathroom, you little bitch,' spat Helen. I knew what was coming to me – she didn't even have to tell me the drill any more. I took off my clothes and waited in the freezing room, clad only in my threadbare underwear. I waited and waited. Shivering. Dying inside at the thought of losing my precious, wonderful Auntie Nellie. 'Over the bath,' snapped Helen as she came into the room. 'Bend right over. And shut your fucking face.' As the tawse railed down on the pathetic bits of flesh stretched over my bones, I knew the outside of my body was aching – but it was nothing compared to the ache I felt inside. Helen left me there, with a list of warnings. 'You're on "no rations". Don't even think of food. You don't speak unless you're spoken to. You don't move unless you have permission. In fact, you don't even fucking breathe unless I say you can.' She also informed me that a couple of weeks had been added to my 'sentence'. This was a strange notion of hers which allowed her to maintain the pretence that this was all about basic discipline, not child abuse. Those days, I was under a constant sentence from Helen. Whenever she claimed I had done something else 'wrong', another week or so would be added. I never knew what the total sentence was and I would never dare ask.

I was graciously allowed to go back to my bedroom, my freezing tiny body cultivating yet more cuts and bruises. Helen screeched at me to stand facing the wall without moving. As I counted the roses on the wallpaper, tracing the pattern over and over again with my eyes, things seemed more hopeless than ever. I had always had Auntie Nellie to dream of before – but she was gone. I was bitterly cold, starving, hurting inside and out, completely alone, and I had lost the one individual who had actually treated me as a person. When my Dad came home, the yelling started again – this time with Gordon smirking in the background. My Dad said he was going to disown me for bringing such shame on the family, but I knew they were only words.

I stood there in that room, listening to the insults, feeling the pain creep through my body, watching Gordon sneer at me, and I vowed to myself that one day – one day – I would be a person of whom Auntie Nellie would be proud. They wouldn't crush me; they wouldn't take away what she had instilled in me, no matter how hopeless it seemed.

I never saw my Auntie Nellie again. She died a few years later, and it came to light at the reading of her will that she had planned to leave everything to me, until that fateful day. She may not have bequeathed me her house or its contents, but her efforts were not in vain. Apart from the obvious bequest of a love of books and a thirst for knowledge, Elizabeth Ewart left me with hope and a yearning to discover myself, to find the woman she thought that little girl could become. She made me realise the value of what each of us holds in our heart, no matter how bleak things become.

Auntie Nellie had gone. I was more alone than ever. All I was left with were her words. 'Books are the key to knowledge, and knowledge is the key to life itself.'

And that alone would become enough to save me.

Chapter Nine

❦

PARTY TIME

1968

AUNTIE NELLIE LEFT ME with an amazing legacy. I think about her much more than I think about Helen Ford, and I actively try to put the good stuff from Nellie way ahead of the bad stuff from Helen. As well as the emotional support and intellectual stimulation my father's aunt gave me, she also provided a practical release. When she died, her huge collection of books was given to our family. Of course, this meant nothing to Helen. The books were worthless to her as reading material; she would never have considered actually using them – the only surprise is that she didn't try to sell them as soon as they arrived. For me, they were a lifeline. Naturally, they weren't given to me. They were stored in the boys' room and I had to access them surreptitiously. My bed was next to a wall, against a door, on the other side of which was Simon's bed. We couldn't use the door properly, but Simon could open it a tiny bit and pass books through to me. Until then, I had been in total despair. Then I discovered this amazing, magical world. I had my escape and Nellie had given it to me.

I adored the musty smell of each new book that came through that tiny passage towards me. I loved the avenues which were opened up each time a new adventure began. I could be transported to a world in which orphans won and young girls conquered their oppressors. I went on travels and had such experiences, even while stuck in a room with little light, no door handle, and an ogress outside. I learned to cope by living in a fantasy world. Books were all I had – they were the saviours of my childhood. On a daily basis, whenever possible, I would disappear into a story, becoming an intrinsic part of the plot, the scheme and the drama. Reading took me so very far away from my life as I was living it. I began to draw the scenes of the story on the blank pages at the beginning or end of the book, making it all as real as possible. My absolute favourite was *Little Women*, and I could reread it a hundred times without being bored, each time a new character appealing, each time a new story thread reeling me in.

Of course, Helen couldn't bear it. On the occasions when she did catch me reading, I always thought that would be the last book I'd ever see. But something stopped her from getting rid of them, burning them or selling them – I can only assume my Dad played some part because I would hear them arguing about it, and I would be given another reprieve. Reprieve in the sense that the books would stay on Simon's side of the door, but I would be beaten senseless for yet another rule transgression.

Things hadn't changed for the better in Edina Place. I was still starving, still beaten, still neglected, humiliated and unloved. But now I had my books, I had my other world. Was that why Helen decided to make things even worse?

ॐ

I know that, to a lot of people, I am nothing more than a category. I was an abused child. I am an adult living with the memories of that abuse. To some, I am a victim. To others, I am a survivor. But behind each label, behind each story, is an individual. And for this individual, the memories of the sexual abuse I suffered, endured and moved on from have created the adult I am today. I defy anyone sexually abused as a child to claim that the abuse has had no effect on the way they have developed as a sexual being. However, it is only as I have begun to revisit my past that I have started to realise fully just how significant this aspect of my earlier life is to the person I now am. I wanted to say that it didn't matter. I wanted to claim that it was of no consequence – but that is a façade that takes either too much stupidity or too much effort to maintain. I do feel that I have, at many points in my life, been in denial regarding this part of my history. What those men did, as much as what my stepmother did, has made me. I now owe it to myself to face that.

I'll never forget the day it started. I was a resilient child – I had to be – but even I didn't think things could get worse. By this time in my life, I was seeing some patterns to what was happening to me. The beatings, the physical abuse, the mental torture, the humiliation always happened when my Dad was at work and when Helen had one of her parties. These parties took place during the day; they had to as that was when she knew she had a free run. I don't know when the parties started – they seemed to be going on all the time. Helen loved the attention and the noise. She appeared to revel in it, and she never needed a reason for one of her 'events'. She always had people coming round, and she seemed to know everyone in the Easter Road area and Leith. All I do know is that I was starting to dread the days when Helen would get dressed up, and I would often see this if it was a school holiday or if I was being kept off school for no real reason. She would get her make-up on, struggle into a miniskirt, and start boozing in preparation. Carlsberg Special Brew was her drink of choice. The beer was stronger than most others, beloved of alcoholics and down-and-outs, and a sure sign that Helen was ready to party. The first time I was sexually abused at one of her parties, I was so confused and bewildered that I'm not entirely sure I knew what happened.

'Get to your room, bastard!' she had shrieked at me just after lunch. 'And fucking stay there!' I was happy to go. Her parties were loud and rowdy. I didn't know the people who came because I was always in the boxroom. Quite content, I left her, glad to escape without a cuff to the side of my head. I sneaked into my room. It was freezing and it was dreary, but it was mine. I settled down under the covers to read *Little Women*, always my favourite, always the one I wanted to go back to.

I could hardly concentrate. I wanted to get lost in my book, the way I always did, but it was so loud. The party was in full swing, even though it was the middle of the afternoon, and Helen was already knocking back the Special Brew. I could hear Frank and Nancy Sinatra singing 'Something Stupid'. I could hear laughter and shrieking and high spirits. It always felt vaguely threatening, but at least I was in my room, even if it was dark and miserable. I could hear cans being opened and chattering going on. I could hear men. I could hear Helen.

As always, I was aware of everything. When I moved around in my room, or read, I would watch for changes in light and shadow at the little gap at the bottom of my door, which would warn me she was coming. This day, I could hear the movement of more than one person. I knew something was going to happen. I just felt it in the pit of my stomach, in every part of me.

There was hushed whispering outside my door.

They weren't moving down the hall.

They weren't going away.

Oh my God – was she bringing someone else in to batter me? Was there to be more torture?

I couldn't yet see the shadow of feet at the door, but I put my book into its hiding place under my mattress then sat back, fully upright, assuming Helen would be in any second.

I hadn't done anything! I hadn't even asked to go to the toilet! I knew by now that it didn't actually matter – I never *did* anything, but it didn't stop me getting beaten.

I heard a man and a woman outside.

I heard some muffled giggling.

Then the door handle turned and the door opened slightly.

I didn't have a handle on my side of the door, but others were free to come and go as they wanted from the other side. My privacy didn't matter. What was going on this time? I knew by now it wasn't just Helen. The movements of the handle were too slow. There was no anger behind them, just wariness. If it had been my stepmother, she would have been in the room by now, and my face would already be stinging from her slaps.

Someone came into the room.

A man?

Someone else pushed him in slightly and closed the door behind him.

I saw his silhouette. Definitely a man.

Then he spoke. Softly.

'Donna?' he said. Why did he question who I was? There couldn't be any doubt. Anyone coming into that room would know it was mine. She would tell them and she was in control of everything. He repeated my name as he shuffled towards me. 'Donna?' he said into the darkness that belied the daylight outside.

I was terrified. He must have known because he made a pathetic excuse to reassure me with his words.

'Donna? Don't worry. Don't be scared, hen. Everything will be fine. Nothing to worry about.'

His words had the opposite effect. I didn't recognise his voice. I could hear the party going on and, for a moment, thought of shouting, screaming, for help. Instantly, I realised that would be futile. Who would help me? I listened as the laughing and the music carried on, and this man kept telling me not to worry as he took tiny soft steps towards me.

I heard a voice in the lobby. Was someone out there listening? What for? Was this a dare? Was it all some sort of joke?

The man got closer and closer, finally reaching my bed. He sat down. His eyes were obviously adjusting to the dim light, but it didn't matter as he was in a more powerful position anyway – he knew my name; I had no idea who he was.

He reached out.

He touched my hair.

He stroked it.

He was on the edge of my bed and he started saying something. I couldn't focus, couldn't work out the words. I knew this was dangerous. But what could I do? I couldn't speak. I knew I daren't speak. I thought it was best just to let him ramble on – what was he saying?

'Donna? Can you hear me? Are you listening? I was just saying – well, I've seen you around, Donna. I've been watching you. You're an awfully pretty wee lassie, Donna. A real stoater.'

What? What? Why was he lying? Was it to distract me? I wasn't pretty. I was ugly. An ugly little bitch. A bastard.

'Have you got a boyfriend, Donna? Have you got a young man that you – well, that you get close to?'

I was barely nine years old, I rarely got out of the house, and he was wanting to know if I got up to anything with boys? Was he mad?

'You must get told how gorgeous you are all the time, Donna. I bet the lads can't keep their hands off you. You're a real wee tease, Donna, aren't you?'

He went on and on. It didn't make sense. What was he up to? I kept shaking my head to everything he asked me. He kept repeating himself.

You're very pretty.

I've seen you around.

You must have a boyfriend.

You're very pretty.

I've had my eye on you.

You're very pretty.

You're very pretty.

You're very pretty.

I wanted him to go away. He was scaring me now. His words were taking on a panicky tone. He started tugging at the covers, pulling them down off me. I held on to them, trying to keep myself covered. It was a battle – an unfair one. A nine-year-old, terrified, starved little girl against a grown man? No contest.

Then things changed. He wasn't soft and placatory any more. His face came right up to mine and he said the words which terrified me: 'You don't want me to tell Helen you've been a bad girl, do you?'

I was shocked. He was threatening me. He must have known what she was like, what she did to me, to know that he could use that against me. As I turned all of this over in my mind, he yanked the bedclothes off in one swift move. I was shivering.

He stayed close to me. Leered over my face and, with one hand, pulled my pants down.

I tried with all my might – although there was precious little of it – to keep my legs closed. Every time I made some feeble attempt to do so, he prised them open again. I tried to focus on details as I had always done, but the overwhelming stench of beer and cigarettes was stronger than anything else. I tried to think about anything – my books, music, food.

But I knew what he was doing.

He carried on prodding and pulling and poking. He was thrusting his fingers into me and I was in agony. He ripped my pants off as I cried and cried and cried. It hurt and it was horrible. I knew he shouldn't be doing it and I knew no one would care.

He kept telling me I was pretty, that he had been watching me, that I was a good girl. He pulled my hand and dragged it towards his penis. He moved it backwards and forwards, faster and faster, and kept sticking his own fingers of his other hand between my legs. I was trying to shift away but he was telling me to stay still. He was whispering things I didn't understand, words I had never heard. Then, all of a sudden, his breathing got faster, and he was telling me I was a good girl, a good girl, then he had this horrible, sticky, silly mess coming out of him.

Then he stopped.

He got up and wiped himself on his shirt tail.

I pulled my pants on and the covers up.

He started speaking again. He stroked my hair, put his fingers to his lips and said, 'Ssshh! That'll be our wee secret, won't it now? Good girl.'

He headed towards the door. I expected him to walk out but, of course, there was no handle. He tapped gently on the door and someone opened it. Someone had been there all along! Someone knew! I heard a female voice whispering as he left, and two sets of footsteps going down the hall back to the party.

I was weeping so much that I was terrified Helen would hear me. I was really hurting between my legs and I still had the silly sticky stuff on my hand. I knew there would be no point telling anyone. No one cared. I sat there in the dark wondering what made me so bad. I saw the girls at school with ribbons in their hair and mummies picking them up and longed for just a tiny bit of that. Now, when someone told me I was a good girl, a pretty girl, it came with all this pain. What was wrong with me? Had my own mummy known I was going to be bad? Is that why she left?

However bad I had felt up to now, Helen made sure I could only feel worse. The man who had abused me that day would be back. As would others. The parties became more frequent, and the abuse commonplace. Whenever there was a party, I knew when there would also be an assault on me. The paedophiles whom she presented me to had their own code – they would enter the house in Edina Place with three rings of the doorbell. When the parties started, I'd listen out for the 'special' rings – and break into a sweat when I knew one of them had arrived. As an adult, even having blocked out most of the abuse in order to function, I would have recurring nightmares in which I could hear the doorbell ringing. Three times. This was always so real that I would wake in a panic, and rush to the door to discover there was no one there. It was only when I began to research my past that this, and many other triggers, went off, reminding me of what had happened.

I now wonder how I could ever have forgotten.

Chapter Ten

ৼ

THE BARBER

1968

THERE SEEMED TO BE no end to the situations Helen could contrive in her quest to make my life even more intolerable. And now the sexual abuse had started, life was darker than ever before. Until recently, the only way I could deal with what I endured was to bury huge parts of my past, but the trial forced me to confront things I had tried to forget. The abuse I suffered was so frequent and so much a part of my life that it can be quite difficult to disentangle specific incidents – how many parties there were or how many times I was beaten are questions I can never answer. But some events, some characters, are horrifically clear.

There would occasionally be times when Helen was 'nice' to me. Her version of niceness wasn't quite what most people managed, or even aspired to. There would never be any hint of selflessness, any notion of kindness for its own sake. There was only one reason for her to be nice to the 'little witch' – when she wanted something. Everything that was given to me as a treat was done so as if it were a huge sacrifice on her part. At rare times, I would be allowed to get up from my bed, get out of my room and get dressed in what passed for my good clothes.

I knew it was always for a reason. There had never been a

time when it hadn't been, so my response was mixed. Of course I enjoyed the chance of moving out of my prison, but I also knew there would be a price. And I knew what that price was likely to be. I came to dread these special 'kindnesses', the times when I was fully aware that escaping from where I was left to rot also meant that hell was just around the corner.

Helen had a hierarchy of demands. At the lower end, she would want me to do fairly basic things for her. In a normal relationship, in a normal family, these activities wouldn't be a problem, but nothing was free or meaningless when Helen was around. Sometimes I would only be sent to do the shopping, or 'messages' as we called it. This wasn't particularly arduous, and neither was taking Andrew for a walk to get him to sleep. When she asked me to get some milk, or take the baby out for five minutes, there was such a bland normality to reconcile with what happened at other times that confusion threatened to overwhelm me.

As I did these mind-numbing, day-to-day tasks, I wanted to scream at people: 'Look at me! Look at this little girl being sent out for a loaf of bread! Look at this child in your shop, walking past you, standing at your side in a queue!' But no one ever really saw me. They didn't see the emaciated frame, the bruises, the pain in my eyes. I was just another kid.

At other times, I would be sent out because a visit from the social workers was on the cards. Perhaps there were times when Helen herself felt I was a loose cannon. Some visits would have me present – from Easter Road onwards, I had been warned as to how I should behave when social workers, Barnardo's representatives or nuns came round. Other times, she simply didn't trust me to be there and I was sent out – I have wondered whether she was so sure of her complete power over me that she could guarantee I would never say anything to incriminate her. Perhaps she was less sure than I thought, and that was why I was sometimes sent on a tenuous errand and told to keep out of the way for the afternoon. But did those social workers never think to ask where I was, or to wait another five minutes, or to suspect that there was something wrong when one of the children they were there to see was absent on the very day they called?

Alongside these mundane reasons for being allowed out were the times when I was allowed to sit in the living room with the rest of the family. This was such a novelty that it remains with me to this day. And, of course, there were the occasions on which she would 'let' me brush her hair. Of all the non-violent, non-abusive things Helen could think of, this was the worst. I despised her so much that the very thought of touching her in any way made me nauseous. I can revisit the smell to this day – the staleness of her scalp, the way it stayed with me long after the chore had been completed. Helen believed the granting of this favour to be a special treat, and, as she passed the hairbrush to me, I could feel the bile rising in my stomach. I didn't want to be anywhere near her, and yet here I was trapped in some awful parody of domesticity, making my stepmother look 'lovely'.

As an adult, I see the irony in that. Helen's transparent little favours – a trip to buy some provisions, five minutes in the living room, a feeble attempt at getting the tangles out of her hair – were always a means of getting her own way. There was another category entirely, which I came to view with blind panic, errands which had nothing to do with shopping but everything to do with her continued exploitation of me.

☞

As you walked around the corner from Edina Place and our house, there was a whole host of shops on Easter Road. It was a typical 1960s street. Just past the Tiffin Café, next to the fishmonger's, was one particular shop.

The barber's.

It was a traditional shop front, right down to the red and

white striped pole outside. But I doubt anyone could have really guessed what was waiting for me in there on the days I was sent on an errand. Behind such a warming, stereotypical exterior, I was to have some of my most appalling experiences.

On my first visit to the barber, Helen asked me to take a message. Her version of 'asking' was never quite as pleasant as the word might suggest.

'Ugly! Get your arse through here!' she called to me in the boxroom. It was teatime on a weeknight, probably around five o'clock, as she passed me a piece of paper with something written on it. 'Take this. Don't read it – you know better. Take it, get along to the barber's, wait … for a bit, then get your lazy, ugly, bastarding self back here before I leather you.'

I'd been to this barber's before when my brothers were taken for their 'short back and sides', so I knew where it was. I was often given chores such as taking the boys for haircuts, motherly things that needed to be done but which Helen couldn't be bothered with when there were parties to organise and Special Brew to drink. The man who ran the shop also owned it and had spoken to me on haircut days and on seeing me pass his door at other times.

He seemed fine.

He seemed normal.

He seemed nice.

Nothing about his demeanour or words at those times had given me any indication that he was one of Helen's 'special friends'. I don't know whether he was one of the men who regularly came to her parties. I suppose our house was close enough to his shop for him to nip out even during work days, but I found it hard to match up the faces of those who came to Helen's parties with those I saw out in the real world, in day-to-day life.

The Barber – I don't know what his real name was – to me was just a rather small man with glasses and slicked-back

Brylcreemed hair. He wore the typical white jacket of barbers at that time, waist-length with four patch pockets, two on the chest and two at waist level. He kept combs and scissors in the chest pockets and always managed to produce a sweetie or two from the others.

Nothing unusual.

Children like men like that.

I took the piece of paper from her – what could have been written there? – and ran round the corner. I belted past Mieles, the chip shop, where the aroma of freshly cooked chips would almost make me faint with hunger. Plenty of times I had picked up discarded newspaper wrappings with the remnants of someone's supper and hungrily wolfed down whatever was left. I would lick the sauce or vinegar dregs from the packets left lying around on the streets and thank my lucky stars for the wastefulness of others. On this day, however, I didn't have time for such luxuries. I had been told to hurry by Helen – the Barber couldn't wait. Thoughts were buzzing through my head – was he to come to our house to cut the boys' hair? Was a party planned that he was invited to? Was Helen selling something else off and telling him to collect it? None of them came even close to anticipating what was ahead of me.

I went straight into the Barber's shop, pushing the half-glazed door, ringing the door bell as I did so – no point standing on ceremony when I was on what seemed to be such an important mission. Even though it wasn't that late, there were no customers inside – just him. I told the man I had a message from Helen, which I handed straight over. As soon as I gave him the piece of paper, he walked to the door and put the lock on. I wondered what Helen had written. That everything was fine? That it was all sorted? That he could do what he wanted because Helen had authorised it?

He was looking at the note and I was looking at him. His baggy grey flannels were hanging down from under his jacket as he started talking to me. 'Helen says you're to help me clear up,' he said. I was even more confused. Was that it? Why was I to help out today? Was it going to be a regular job? Why hadn't Helen told me? Was I going to get a sweetie, or was I to be cheated of that? I looked around, but everywhere was so clean and tidy that there was nothing for me to help out with. I thought I would try anyway.

'Alright,' I said. 'Where will I start?'

'Just polish the counter,' he answered. 'Just make a good job of that, and then we'll see.'

I started on the job that didn't need doing as he stood and watched.

'Well done, you've made a grand job of that,' I was told after a while. He reached into his pocket – a sweetie! Everything had worked out – although I couldn't understand why I'd had to go through the rigmarole of doing an unnecessary job. Still, I had done what was asked of me. I shouldn't be due a beating for that, maybe just a slap round the head when I got back.

'Would you like a wee shot on the chair, hen?' he asked.

Things were looking up! This was a real treat. A bonus.

The big revolving black leather seat had already been something I'd had a go at when I was in with my brothers. I'd love to have another shot – and on my own this time too! The chair was quite big, and I was, of course, pretty small, smaller even than I should have been at that age, but I could manage to get up onto it myself. The Barber had other ideas – maybe he was just being nice? – and he came over to me, lifting me on to the chair and spinning me round. I was having a bit of fun for once.

As quickly as the spinning had started, it stopped. All of a sudden, the Barber halted the motion of the chair and turned me to face him. He was looking at me squarely in the face. His eyes looked as if they too were twirling, due to his milk bottle lens glasses. I barely knew what was happening, it was so quick.

This nice man with the sweeties in his pocket and the spinning chair put his hands on my knees and let them travel up my legs, lifting my skirt as he did so.

I was terrified.

This wasn't right.

Even I knew that, and I certainly knew it wouldn't stop there. I looked towards the door of the shop but the place was closed down, the blinds pulled so that no one could see out or in. I could hear the traffic on Easter Road go by quite normally. Buses taking people to town, or bringing them back home. Other children walking outside the door, laughing. The chattering of women walking by, their heels clip-clopping, clip-clopping as they passed by.

I tried to push my skirt down to cover myself but he was too strong.

'I'd better go,' I whimpered. One lie to try. 'Helen will be so worried. She'll wonder where I am.'

The Barber laughed. He knew the game a lot better than I did. 'Don't you worry about Helen, hen,' he snorted. 'She knows where you are. Everything will be fine. She knows you're… helping me.'

My heart was pounding. I was dreading what was going to happen next. The Barber tugged and pulled at my pants and forced my skinny legs apart. I was crying and asking him to stop but he wouldn't. He got his penis out and started masturbating whilst forcing his fingers inside me. What was he doing? What was he thinking of?

I was so ashamed. So embarrassed. So full of tears and fear and confusion. It didn't touch him. Perhaps my distress made the experience all the sweeter for him.

'Come on now, stop your greeting. That's me done, now. If you keep crying like that, folk will think there's something wrong. You wouldn't want someone to think there's something wrong, would you? Now, wash your face. Get yourself cleaned up. You'll get a sweetie if you're good.'

He was washing himself as he spoke to me, over the sink where he shampooed hair and shaved people.

Where good people came for their haircuts, where children sat and got ready for their first day at school, where men sat and discussed their weekends and their families.

The Barber had taken just a bit more of my childhood away.

He had his back to me; I wasn't really there any more – not for him. I did as I was told, washed my face and straightened myself up. I looked in the mirror and hated the face that stared back at me, hated the fact that I was the sort of person that had these things done to them, hated the fact that it kept happening. How bad must I be for this to keep going on?

The Barber was finished. He put his hand into his pocket and pulled out a MacCowans penny dainty. The green and white tartan wrapper sat in my hand. 'Eat it now, eat it here,' he said. 'If you keep that until you get home, one of your brothers will have it away quick as a flash. D'you fancy another wee go in the chair?'

I was in a daze. I ate my sweetie and sat in the chair – my reward. I walked home, my helping out over, my errand completed. Who could I tell? Helen? She had sent me there. She knew exactly what was going on. My Dad was on one of his eternal overtime stints. There was no one – and I was beginning to wonder whether anyone would believe me anyway. It seemed so unlikely. I knew the world went on as usual even while I was being abused, so how could I think that the world would even care?

Visits to the Barber became a regular occurrence. Each time I would dread it more, as each time the level of abuse changed. I was never vaginally raped by the Barber, but his attacks were so appalling that I find it hard to think of them, even as an adult. I was raped by other men, but even to this day cannot talk, cannot 'go public' on those particular instances of abuse. Each time the Barber chose what was to happen, and I would never know exactly which part of me he would abuse, which part of me he would attack. After that first time, I never got a sweetie again. I would be sent, *loaned out* and then abused as if it was the most natural thing in the world.

Strangely, it stopped as abruptly as it had started. My brothers still went for haircuts. I still followed them there. But that chapter was over. The Barber was just a normal man again and I was still a bad girl – I was learning.

When I was visited by the police as an adult and told that they were collecting evidence to see whether a case could be brought against Helen, I had very little time in which to give my statement in terms of all the things which had happened in my past. How could I remember it all at once? How could I get it all down into one statement? But the police needed me to give them something. And I did. But the statement they took to the Procurator Fiscal was only a tiny portion of what really went on. By the time I went to court I had remembered so much more. So very, very much more. One of my memories was this one – the Barber. I stood up in the witness box and I told them all about that man. I sat there as lawyers discussed whether it could be included, whether that part of my horror was 'relevant', and I felt as if it was all happening again. I wouldn't be believed, I would have been better to keep quiet as he had warned me. When they came back and told me that it was allowed, it was to be included, I was shocked – someone was finally listening, even if it was decades too late. I was never told whether he was dead or alive, whether he was investigated or not (some things never change). His shop is no longer there but I can see his face clear as day even as I write this.

Chapter Eleven

WHAT UGLY LITTLE GIRLS DESERVE ...

1969–1970

THE PARTIES WENT ON, the horror continued. By now, I knew I was worthless. I knew I was ugly and I knew what being a bastard meant. I also suspected that I was very, very bad indeed. If I wasn't bad, then why was I always being punished? As more and more nameless men abused me, I was starting to face up to something – I meant nothing, I counted for nothing. Everything I thought about myself came from Helen. She made it clear that everything was my fault – I brought it all on myself. I had it all coming to me, in her words.

What happened to me during those years still remains with me – but not always in obvious ways. I don't think anyone could know whether those who have endured child sexual abuse can ever be truly free – psychologically – of their experiences. However, I do know that the physical repercussions of my time with Helen Ford live with me to this day.

I would never dare mention I was ill when I was a child. It wasn't just a sign of weakness; it was a sign of indulgence. Only special people could get ill, because only special people deserved the attention needed to make them better again.

And I, most certainly, was not in that category. I learned the hard way.

One day in Edina Place, when I was about 10 years old, I was on bathroom punishment as usual. But today felt different. I was cold, as always, but was also just as hot. I was shifting so quickly from one extreme to the other that I was confused. One minute I was freezing, shaking and shivering; the next I was burning up, feeling sick and faint. It was during school holidays and I had been there since just after breakfast – other people's breakfast, not mine – and it was now late afternoon. My throat felt as though there was something stuck in it. It was agony – so bad that I knew I needed to risk Helen's anger by telling her something was wrong. I couldn't shout as my throat was too sore, and I realised that I needed to leave the bathroom to let my stepmother know there was something the matter with me. Time was passing. As I stood there, alone, feverish, I could feel myself sway. I just wanted to lie down, but knew that this wasn't allowed. Eventually, I knew I would have to bite the bullet and ask. Ask for help. Ask for permission to go to bed. Shakily, I turned round and took a few faltering steps towards the bathroom door.

I knew that Helen was in the kitchen because I could hear her. I walked, staggered, across the floor, feeling so ill that I was willing to risk challenging her by leaving the bathroom. I stood behind her at the kitchen sink. 'Helen,' I whispered. She whirled round with a dishcloth still in her hand. 'Jesus Christ! What are you doing there, you sneaky little bitch? Crawling up on people when they don't know it.' Her face came closer to mine. 'Defying me. Laughing in my face.' I was nowhere near laughing. I felt as if I could fall down any second.

'Please Helen,' I began. 'I feel really bad.'

'So you should! I'll give you bloody feeling bad. Get back in there now, and don't you dare come out again.' She went back to washing the dishes, assuming that I'd leave and go back to the bathroom.

This was important. She had to know I wasn't making it up. Usually, I'd never stand up to her, but I had to try again. 'Helen, I really think I need to go to bed. I'm all hot and cold. I think I'm going to pass out.'

She turned back round. 'Are you still there, shit for brains?' She walked towards me. When she got up to my face again, she flicked it with the stinking wet dishcloth on the pronouncement of each word. 'Get.' Flick. 'Back.' Flick. 'To.' Flick. 'The.' Flick. 'Fucking.' Flick. 'Bathroom.' Flick.

I stumbled back to my prison. Closed the door. Fell down on my knees to the cold, cold tiles as the sweat lashed over my body. A wave of nausea was flooding over me as a knock came on the door. Had she changed her mind? Was she letting me out?

'Are you okay, diddums?' her voice sing-songed. 'Is precious feeling better now?'

I lifted my throbbing head up.

Why wasn't she coming in, either to help me or taunt me some more?

'I've been thinking. If you're so unwell, the best place for you is in quarantine. Stay there until we all go to bed tonight. Keep away from the rest of us. If you're riddled with something nasty, I don't want me or Gordon or Andrew to catch it, you filthy little cow.'

Hours passed as I lay there on the tiles, feeling freezing cold one minute and boiling hot the next.

Once more, much later, I plucked up all the courage I had in my scrawny little body. I crawled along the corridor to the room where Helen was. 'Please, Helen,' I croaked. 'Please, help me, I feel awful. Please can I go to my bed? I'll be good. I'll be quiet.' She turned the television off. Stared at me. Then she opened her mouth and bawled as loudly as she could. 'Get out! Get out of here! You've no right to be here! Get back on punishment! Go! Go! Go!'

She made me stand there all evening. Every now and again, as

I drifted in and out of things, I could hear her coming along the corridor, checking up on me. After a while, I realised everyone had gone to bed. My Dad was out, working overtime as usual. And me? I thought, I really thought, that I was going to die. Eventually Helen went to bed too – I heard her come out of the living room and go down the lobby into her bedroom. She didn't bother to check up on me. She knew that I'd still be in there, still 'on punishment'. Finally, I couldn't bear it any more. I staggered out of the bathroom, and sheepishly knocked on her bedroom door. I heard nothing. I knocked again. Still nothing. I opened the door a tiny bit, just a crack. 'Helen,' I whispered. 'Helen, can I please go to bed?' A whirlwind flew at me, knocking me back. She must have been sitting in there waiting for me to request this most outrageous of privileges. 'Bed? Bed? You've got some brass fucking neck, haven't you?' she screamed. I was sweating through my temperature as she started hitting me. She was a mad vision in her slippers and dressing gown, lashing out, knocking me off the wall, slapping my head from one side to another. 'Ill? I'll give you bloody ill! You'll know what ill is when I've finished with you!' I ran back into the bathroom, still pleading for a doctor, and closed the door behind me. She followed me in, absolutely berserk, and continued the beating.

Finally, she seemed to run out of energy and went back to her bedroom. I knew I couldn't even afford the luxury of slumping to the floor, despite my desperate need to do so. If she came back and caught me slacking off, who could tell what she might be capable of? I stood there as long as I could, but I must have fainted, must have lost consciousness, because I remember coming round on the floor to find her standing over me, yelling: 'You! Get to your bed, now! And don't tell your father!'

Next day – actually, probably only some hours later – she came into my boxroom with my Dad. She started fussing around my bed – the pair of them were hardly ever in that room, so it was quite a performance. 'Look, Don,' she said, 'I'm really worried about the bairn. All last night, I kept telling her something was wrong and she needed to let me get the doctor in – but she's that bloody stubborn, she wouldn't hear of it.' My Dad looked at her as if she were Mother Bloody Teresa. 'You're too good, Helen,' he muttered. 'The bairns don't know how much you do for them. Well, it's time you just put your foot down. If you think she needs a doctor, I don't care how pig-headed she is about it – she'll get a doctor.'

So, to the doctor I was taken. Penicillin and rest were prescribed – and Helen made a great show of how tired she was of looking after a sick child; how much easier it would all have been if only I'd got medical attention when she'd first suggested it rather than digging my heels in. Her show was for my Dad, the doctor, the neighbours, anyone who would listen – anyone who would open their ears to her lies, while closing their eyes to the fact that the ill child in front of them couldn't have fought her way out of a paper bag, was covered from head to toe in bruises, and barely had any skin over her bones.

෴

The illnesses I had while a child, and when Helen was around, had repercussions which lasted a lot longer than if I had been properly fed, cared for, and given treatment when I required it. I had constant tonsillitis until I was 12 – at that age, I had my tonsils removed and spent a week in Astley Ainslie Convalescence Unit recovering. I loved that week, because of the attention and the feeling of safety. The nurses used to let me help them with little bits and pieces, and I felt so secure that I never even noticed the pain.

Tonsillitis was one of the more minor problems of my child-hood. Other, more serious, health problems persisted into my adult life. When I was being sexually abused, I was always sore 'down below' and had terrible problems with my 'waterworks' (how strange that, despite the awful things being done to me, I was never allowed to use 'dirty' – that is, proper – words for bodily parts and functions). The fact that I was unable to go to the toilet when I needed to didn't help the situation at all. For as far back as I can remember, from the day of arriving at Easter Road right up to the present, I have had issues with my 'waterworks'. As a child, I wet the bed, and this became a major issue for Helen. I couldn't help it; I was five years old! I'd just come out of care, I wet the bed and, for some reason, she thought this was the end of the world. She got more and more annoyed about it until eventually she started to rub my nose in the sheets in the morning, make me take my wet pants off, rub my face with them, make me put them back on and wear them. It's no surprise that at school I was called pissy pants.

Another one of her remedies for my bed-wetting was to make me strip the bed down to the rubber sheet. I hated that rusty red sheet, stinking of rubber and pee. I'd have to scrub the rubber sheet in the bath, trample the sheets, then wring them before hanging them out to dry in the back green or, if it was raining, on the pulley. As I got older, I would get more and more embarrassed about going to school stinking of piss. I would run to the girls' toilets where I would try to clean myself with the powdery borax soap and dry myself with hard, green paper towels. I even got to the stage of washing my knickers then putting them back on wet. Nothing helped – either with the smell or with my problems with 'normal' toilet behaviour.

I also have the most awful back problems relating directly to the beatings I endured as a child. I remember one occasion in particular when Helen gave me a beating and really damaged my back. We'd just come back from a holiday in Kinghorn – two weeks at a chalet in a holiday camp in Fife. I'd enjoyed it so much as we'd had more freedom there than we were ever allowed at home. I think most of that was due to Helen wanting us out from under her feet, but there was also the fact that my Dad was around for the whole holiday. After breakfast, we'd be shunted out for the day. Simon and I would head off rock-pooling, catching minnows or sticklebacks. We'd go on long expeditions and find caves; we'd jump in the water off the pier.

Most of it was good.

But Helen had packed a little extra in her holiday bag. Her beloved tawse. When my Dad was around, she was okay – but when he went drinking to the clubhouse, she'd get the beating belt out, concentrating on my back as much as possible. Simon and I got a lot more than one leathering on that holiday, reminders that lasted longer than the few happy moments at the rock pools.

Shortly after this holiday, Simon and I got a really bad hiding for an imaginary slight. It was Simon's go first. This was one of Helen's preferred approaches. She made us queue up outside the bathroom door, taking turns, waiting, listening to the other child's cries of pain in anticipation of what was coming our way. Simon was screaming; when it stopped, he came out of the bathroom crying, hugging himself and slouching with pain. He scurried to his room. I was next. I did the usual – held on to the cold bath and listened to Helen's words.

'You know why you're being punished.'

'You know you're bad.'

'You know you deserve it.'

'Say it! Say it! Say you're bad, you deserve this!' she would scream.

Eventually I would.

'I am bad. I deserve to be punished.'

She'd tell me to bend over. Not to move. I'd lean over the bath and wait for the stinging thwack of the belt. But this time, this one time, it wasn't the belt – it was the buckle. I don't know whose belt it was, whose belt she had chosen to beat me with, but it was heavier than usual, and the cumbersome brass buckle on it put me in agony each time it came down as she hit me. I tried my hardest not to show just how much pain I was in, but I failed miserably. My back was aching and I swear I heard a crack. Helen just kept hitting and hitting and shouting and shouting. Eventually she stopped and I hobbled off to my room. The pain was so much worse than I had ever felt from a belt beating before, and I kept hearing the cracking noise, over and over again. Ever since that day my back has troubled me and hurts virtually every day. Years ago, a chiropractor looked at it. He scanned his eyes over the x-rays. 'Have you survived a bad car crash?' he asked. 'No,' I replied. 'Just a bad childhood.'

As I mentioned before, my other most significant health issue relates to my eating habits. I spent years as a child going for days on end without food. As a result, I've been left with an inability to eat normal-sized portions or, indeed, even a full meal. I have to pick and eat small parts of any plateful. It frustrates me and annoys me and is extremely anti-social. When you're invited for a meal, people look, and you can see their eyes questioning. Being small anyway, I'm sure people think I have an eating disorder. In a way I do, but it is not self-imposed. Years of starving have left me this way, and the only way I can compensate is by cooking for other people, which I love.

⚬

I have come to terms with the fact that these things are simply part of me now – but that doesn't stop me questioning how it all happened in the first place. Some of the main questions I have are for Barnardo's. I feel so let down by them. Although they looked after me competently enough while I was at Haldane House, I can't help but blame them for not adequately checking up on what I returned to.

Why did these people not save me? Why did they not do something? They couldn't have known the situation I was going to face, but if they had got us placed elsewhere then maybe Helen would never have got her hands on us. I know it was on the cards because I have read it in old reports. In one it says: 'Unfortunately, neither of their parents seems able to keep in very close touch with the children and we are therefore planning to find a suitable home where they can be fostered, so that this will give them the opportunity of growing up in the environment of a normal happy home, where they will receive every loving care and attention.' The fact that I had been so close to a different life chills me to the bone.

A normal happy home.

Every loving care and attention.

These were things I would dream of for so long. Things I believed I did not deserve. Things that had been within touching distance without me even knowing. There are so many 'what ifs'. What if I had been placed with another family and managed to enchant them so much that they wanted me as their own child? What if I'd had a completely different childhood? How would I have turned out?

I also want to know how on earth teachers could have been so blind to what was going on in front of them every day. As I have said, my first school was Leith Walk Primary, and I started there at the end of the first summer that I returned to stay with my father and stepmother. Did the teachers at that little Victorian school choose to ignore the skinny, terrified little girl who stank of piss? Each day when they patrolled the separated girls' and boys' playgrounds, did they just fail to notice me, isolated, excluded, bruised and starving?

It was my treatment at home that finally brought me to the attention of those who should have looked out for me long before – but it did little good. I had become so obsessed with food that I stole food from the pockets of another child one day. (When Don and Helen found out, it was used as just another excuse to beat me.) This was raised at the court case as evidence of my evil streak – Helen was being tried for procuring us for sexual abuse as children, and lawyers tried to make out that it was all made up because I was the sort of evil kid who lied and stole food! I'll say now what I said under oath – only one type of child steals food, and that is a hungry child. At the time, it was enough to get me sent to an educational psychologist.

The only decent meal I ever got was on a school day. Simon and I were given free school dinners. We were marked out by the pink tickets we held up for all to see and sneer at. All the people who paid for their dinners got first sitting and us paupers went in last. The advantage of last sittings was the opportunity to get 'seconds', even though the favourite dishes had usually been snaffled by the paying diners. I didn't care that we had to be labelled to get free school meals – I still dreamed of them. I looked forward to lunch so much, often anticipating and almost drooling whilst trying to imagine what it would be each day. Would it be mince? Sloppy, dark brown with carrots in, accompanied by a perfect scoop of mashed tatties complete with lumps and black-eyes? Then maybe followed by cake and custard? Whatever was served, I ate every morsel.

Now, thinking back, I have such evocative memories of the dinner hall, the clanking of the aluminium trays, the smell of the hot food which would permeate the corridors from just after playtime. Food meant everything to me at school. I came to school hungry so my mind was on my belly for most of the time. When I got to school in the morning, I thought about when milk would be served. I liked milk time – more so in the winter when it was icy cold – a third of a pint in its little glass bottle with a foil cap. It was someone's job to trek down the long corridor to where the milk was kept and return to the class with the crate. Someone else would then give out the milk which you would sip through a pink plastic straw. As well as using the straws to drink our milk, we would often join them together in three-dimensional geometric shapes, then carefully cover them in coloured cellophane, sometimes sweet wrappers – and hang them haphazardly around the classroom. They looked so beautiful – like jewels or magic lanterns. I vaguely remember being told it had something to do with maths, but to me it was even more evidence that good things came from having a full stomach.

In the early days at Easter Road, I do remember having breakfast most days before leaving for school, usually cornflakes with milk and sugar, or toast. For a little while, I even got a playtime snack – a packet of Golden Wonder crisps or a chocolate biscuit, a Tunnock's caramel log, a caramel wafer or a Blue Riband. I don't know exactly when breakfasts and playtime snacks stopped, but I know it was quite soon after Frances and Simon came home. I had those school lunches to look forward to for such a short while. For some reason – perhaps control, power or pure nastiness – Helen stopped the school dinners and I'd have to run back to the house each day, panting and nervous, maybe late or disappointing her in some way. I'd be given a tiny, snack-size sausage roll from McGill's the baker on a good day and then sent back to school. On a bad day, I got nothing.

So I would have to find ways to get food. I'd pick up sweets off the streets on the way to school or bread that had been left out for the birds. I'd scrounge at playtime, hanging around the kids who had snacks, trying to make them feel guilty and making them hate me even more for my pathetic attempts. I'd take any opportunity to get out of class to rifle through the coats and bags in the cloakroom for food or loose change. If I got a penny, I'd go to the dairy on the way home. The dairy was the little grocer/newsagent/
tobacconist, a tiny shop on our street. I'd buy a penny dainty, just like the one the Barber had given me, in a green and white tartan wrapper. It was a lovely piece of creamy toffee. I'd either eat it straight away or savour it, hiding it in my brown leather school bag to eat in privacy. I knew if Helen came across it I'd be in trouble.

The way I was being treated at home obviously made me the

child I was. In turn, that prevented me from having a normal school life with normal interests and normal friends. I certainly don't really remember having friends at school as such, although I do remember sometimes being 'cawed in' at the skipping in the playground if they were short, and even being allowed to hold an end of the rope on special occasions. Even though I was an outsider, I loved watching the games and singing the songs. When I first started school and Helen was nicer than she became, I played a bit and got to join in. As time went on, however – and I turned up to school smellier, scruffier, more tired, hungry, withdrawn and undoubtedly stranger – I became an easy target to pick on.

As time went on, the knot of tension I felt in my stomach at the prospect of going home, also began to apply to school. I did enjoy some aspects of it, though, particularly history and geography and anything that involved drawing a picture to illustrate work. I loved it when we did a project on the Bayeux tapestry and made a collage. We once got the opportunity to learn French but it didn't last long. I was fascinated by the strange-sounding words and mesmerised by the French teacher, her stories of France and how exotic it all sounded. I liked music and remember our music teacher very clearly. A big part of the reason I liked her was that she reminded me of Auntie Nellie, as she had the same school-marm look with tweed skirts and sensible black lace-up shoes. She made us sing with a round mouth, twirling our finger in our mouth while reciting the scale to ensure we kept our lips in a perfect circle as we sang 'Greensleeves' and 'Early One Morning'.

I also liked writing – it was close to art, which was to become my life – and looked forward to practising my handwriting with a proper fountain pen and writing the alphabet over and over in perfect italics. I hated the times tables and despaired of being asked to stand up and recite what we were expected to learn in maths that day. Numbers bored me and didn't make sense –

mental arithmetic was just hell. Of course, I already knew that reading was a delight. I started off with the 'Janet and John' books, and it wasn't long before I was looking for more and more challenging scripts. I always put my hand up first in spelling but I was never first in line when it came to sports. I was always cold so I would get as near as I could to the radiator and huddle in doorways in the playground rather than run around.

Christmas was the best time at primary school. The gym would be festooned with paper decorations and a huge 'real' tree with twinkling, sparkling, shimmering baubles and tinsel. There was a school party and we'd all gather in the big hall where we'd career up and down the wooden floor doing the 'Grand Old Duke of York', the 'Dusty Bluebells', the 'Farmer's in his Den', followed by a tea of miniature egg sandwiches, sausage rolls, sweet sticky cakes and orange squash. Santa would visit, we'd all sing 'We Wish You a Merry Christmas' then it would all be over. I wished I could take it home with me and felt sick to my stomach when it ended.

꙳

Those were my days, my school memories, but nothing was really separate from what was happening with Helen. I hated home time. I'd start watching the clock just before the bell was due to ring and begin to get really anxious if people started mucking about and there was a chance I'd be late home. I knew Helen would watch the clock and I'd be in big trouble if I was late. I'd get out of school and run as hard as I could, my chest burning with the exertion and my stomach doing somersaults. I'd be relieved if I got home and was only sent to my room. Sometimes I'd be told to stand in the lobby or bathroom and wait; wait to see what she was going to do that day, what she had in store for me. On very, very rare occasions – maybe if she'd had a few cans of Special Brew – she would tell me to get changed and go and play until I was told to come in. On these days, it didn't matter what the weather was like; I just took the chance and did it. Often I'd be called in just in time to do the dishes, tea already having been eaten in my absence, because I didn't matter.

It was just an endless round of starvation, beatings, abuse and cruelty. It beggars belief that I was finally sent to a child psychologist and yet they uncovered nothing. I would have thought it would have taken any decent professional about 10 minutes to work out what was going on, yet I was sent back to Helen time and time again. And each day, it seemed, she thought up new horrors for me. By the time we moved to Edina Place, the social work visits seemed cursory. Helen always told them how awful and evil this ugly little girl was. On top of that, Frances, Simon and I were all told exactly what to say.

Helen had three brass monkey ornaments on the mantelpiece – one with its ears covered, one with its mouth covered, one with its eyes covered. 'Look at them,' she'd hiss before any official visit. 'That's what you lot need to remember – get that in your thick skulls. Hear no evil. Speak no evil. See no evil.' She glowered at me – her particularly despised stepchild. 'You. Don't forget. Don't forget those monkeys. And don't EVER forget that I'm watching you more closely than anyone.'

When the social workers came, the three of us would stand in front of them as they asked us questions. Helen would stand behind them, squinting at us, promising us without words just what would happen if we said a word to shatter the myth of the perfect stepmother. And those monkeys. They terrified me then, and I still break out in a sweat if I see a similar trio to this day.

Helen would never voluntarily give me anything good in my life – however, on one occasion, she slipped up.

I hated Gordon. He was not the little brother I had hoped for. He had become his mother's son. He had lost me my Auntie Nellie, and he treated me like shit. I'd never become attached to Andrew because I'd learned my lesson with Gordon; I chose to avoid Helen's youngest for fear that he would turn on me too. I had closed myself off to her children. I didn't trust them because they came from her and she was the source of my hell.

But then she had another baby.

She had Karen.

จ

I didn't even know she was pregnant. I always kept my eyes away from her when I could, looking only when there was no other option, so I didn't see the growing belly. She was always complaining about being tired, so I wouldn't have noticed any difference there either.

One afternoon, we came back to the house to find my Dad at home. This in itself was unusual enough, but when he told the three boys and me to go to our rooms and stay there (Frances had gone by this time), without any shouting, it did seem a little different. I wasn't about to pry – it was bonus enough that I wasn't being hit. The day dragged on. I heard some shouting, some moaning. Nothing different there. Helen was always shouting. There was often moaning coming from her bedroom too – although usually when my Dad wasn't there. It did go on for an awfully long time though.

Then the doorbell went.

This terrified me.

Usually when Helen sent me to my room, and she made that strange moaning noise, I waited on the bell ringing. Although it was unlikely to be one of the men who abused me because they didn't do that when my Dad was around, I still felt apprehensive. If there was a special coded ring, I knew it would be someone coming for me, someone coming to use me with Helen's permission as part of her party afternoons. But this time, although I heard a man's voice, he didn't come for me. We all stayed in our rooms for ages before my Dad finally said we could come out and go to the loo if we wanted. I remember we all rushed along at the same time and we all stopped just inside the door as we pushed in together.

'Eurgh! What's that?' shouted Gordon, pointing at the bath.

Andrew joined in, making pretend retching noises and shouting, 'Blood! Blood!'

I looked in. The old, stained potty we had was full of some horrible thing – all red, bloody and lumpy. I had no idea what a placenta was, so didn't have a clue what I was looking at.

My Dad pushed past us, grabbed the potty up, shouting, 'Never you bloody mind what it is! Just get on with whatever you need to do and we'll tell you later.'

Later came.

We were ushered into Helen and Don's bedroom where she sat, in a nightie, holding a baby.

She looked quite happy.

'Come and say "hello" to your new sister,' she said. 'This is Karen.' She looked straight at me. 'Isn't she lovely? Isn't she just a beautiful little girl? Just what a little girl should be.'

I walked over, expecting to see a horned devil, another evil spawn. I wasn't prepared, even then, for what I felt. I was 10 years old, and as I looked at this newborn child, I felt more love than I had ever known before. I wanted to rip her out of Helen's arms, to run away with her, protect her for ever. Part of me felt so scared – another girl. Would she face the same fate as me? I knew that skinny as I was, weak as I was, I would do all in my power to stop that.

As the days went on, additional parts of the picture became clearer. I heard others talking about how good my Dad was being, how not many men would stand by their wives in his position. It finally clicked. He wasn't Karen's Dad. Once I realised that, I realised more. I knew who her Dad was. There was one man who had never touched me, who used to hang around a lot. Whenever Helen dragged me to the shops, I always knew if we were going to bump into Lenny because she would make a special effort with her hair, make-up and clothes. She always smiled more around him, and put on her fake personality. He was nice to me too – although that was the last thing I wanted. I remembered a time when we met him in a shop in Easter Road.

'Hello, wee Donna,' he had said, ruffling my hair.

I felt Helen wince beside me as she tried to keep the smile plastered on her face.

'How are you, then? Having a nice day? Keeping yourself busy?'

I didn't know what to answer – I knew I wouldn't be allowed to say anything.

'Cat got your tongue?' asked Helen, knowing full well that it was fear of her that kept me silent. 'She's pig ignorant this one,' she laughed, her face contorting into what she thought was a seductive look rather than a grimace.

Stop. Stop talking to me now, I willed Lenny Crooks.

If you keep talking to me, keep being nice to me, keep giving me attention – I'll pay for it later. I'll pay for it so hard.

But Lenny Crooks couldn't read my mind.

He kept talking.

Kept ruffling my hair.

Then he said the fatal words.

'She's a bonny wee thing, Helen, isn't she?'

I stopped hearing things after that. I knew what was going to happen. She finished her conversation with Lenny and we went home.

She didn't say a word.

She got the tawse.

She stripped me.

She whipped me.

She finally stopped long enough to get her breath and send me naked and bleeding to the bathroom where I stood alone, freezing, starving, until the next morning. For being a 'bonny wee thing'.

The man who had unwittingly caused that was Karen's father.

๛

Through Karen I learned that I could love another person, but I also learned the fear which comes from that. In the event, Helen didn't care for her and she thankfully left when Karen wasn't much more than a baby.

In my new little sister (which was how I thought of her, even though we had absolutely no blood tie), I had the baby dolly I had always hoped for. Even though I was now 10, I still had dreams of the Tiny Tears I had wanted since I left Barnardo's.

In the days leading up to the first Christmas after Karen was born, Helen sidled up to me. 'Well, Donna,' she started. 'What are you hoping Santa brings you this year?' It must be a joke, I thought. Other years, I was lucky if I got a packet of crayons – I got some basic stuff she would need to buy me anyway, but nothing 'frivolous', nothing like the gifts lavished on Gordon and Andrew. I didn't know what to say. Was it a trick? Probably, but I couldn't help myself from telling the truth. Even with Karen around, I still wanted a Tiny Tears – and I told her.

'Is that right? Well ...' she paused as if thinking. 'We'll just have to see what we can do.'

For the next few weeks, I could hardly sleep. There was hope. There really was hope. And on Christmas morning, I could hardly believe my eyes. There, under the pathetic tree, was a box.

A Tiny Tears shaped box.

With my name on it.

For the first time I could remember, there was a beautifully wrapped present, and a tag which said, in big letters:

To Donna
Merry Christmas!!!!!
Xxxxxxxxx

It didn't matter that it didn't say from 'Mum and Dad' – that would be too much to hope for. What did matter was that she was there. My dolly was there. Oh, I would love her so much! I was already thinking how much comfort she would bring me. I would get through things with that dolly to hold and cuddle.

Helen was really getting into the Christmas spirit. She was laughing and jiggling Karen on her hip. 'Come on, everyone,' she called to the others, who were concentrating on their gifts. 'Stop what you're doing and watch Donna open her BIG present! Watch her open just what she deserves.'

Gordon and Andrew moaned a bit, but came over. My Dad was there too. I didn't lift the box up; it was too precious. I left it on the floor, and gingerly took up a corner of paper. I tore a little corner off the wrapping – was it all going to be a disappointment?

I could barely contain myself.

I read the words 'TINY TEARS' out of the corner I had ripped.

I felt faint.

It was real.

SHE was real!

Laughing, hysterical with happiness, I ripped the rest of the paper off.

And sat.

And looked.

And wanted to die.

I heard Helen laughing maniacally behind me.

Gordon shrieking and even Dad laughing too.

And I looked at the box. The Tiny Tears box.

The empty Tiny Tears box.

134

'There you go, Donna!' she cackled. 'There's your present! Enjoy it!'

I looked round to see her wave a hand at me, tears of joy running down her face.

That was my Christmas. That was my gift.

Karen got the doll, although I never saw her with it.

I got an empty box.

Everything an ugly little girl deserved.

Chapter Twelve

ঽ

Blind Jimmy

1969

HELEN'S DEMANDS CONTINUED. There was always something else that she wanted from me – whether it was just for me to stand there as a punchball or act as a 'thing' for her to exercise her temper on, there was no end to the reasons she found for me to be at her beck and call. The parties were part of that – but so were the 'errands' she contrived.

One holiday afternoon, I had managed to escape my stepmother's fists and tongue for a few peaceful hours. I could never relax entirely, but to be left alone in my room was the most I could hope for. I had spent the morning reading my books and thinking about my Auntie Nellie. The rest of the day – even with its isolation and loneliness, even with an empty stomach and a body covered in bruises from my last beating – would have been close to perfect for me if I didn't see Helen until I went to bed that night.

My stepmother had other ideas. She was always offering me to neighbours and cronies to help out. Of course, that 'offering' was even more obscene, more perverted since the parties had become established, but Helen also had what I thought of as a more innocuous side. I was always being sent to do cleaning for people, to help out with baby-sitting, to get their shopping. So it was no surprise when she shouted for me that day.

'Get your lazy little arse through here,' she squawked from the lobby as she passed my room. 'I've got a message for you to run. Blind Jimmy needs a hand with his shopping and you're doing bugger all, so get round there and help the poor old man.'

Blind Jimmy's home was a few streets away from us, a couple of doors down from where Helen had originally lived with her parents. He was old and he was smelly, though I did feel quite sorry for him. He lived on his own, and I assumed that because he couldn't see and couldn't get about very well, he had no idea that he and his house were in such a state. But my sympathy didn't mean that I enjoyed being around him. I bit back my comments and looked at the list Helen gave me – McKellar's the butcher's for his meat and McGill's the bakers for his bread. A straightforward list; I'd get through it in no time.

'Where's the money?' I asked.

'In Blind Jimmy's pocket I suppose,' Helen answered. 'You've to take him with you. Get your ugly little gob round to his flat and go round the shops with him.'

I followed her instructions. Blind Jimmy barely spoke to me as we went up and down Easter Road getting everything on the list. The old man walked with a limp and tapped his white stick against the walls and lamp posts as we went from shop to shop. In every place, he'd say what he wanted without a 'please' or 'thank you', then drag a filthy old grey hankie out of his trouser pocket. The hankie was knotted tightly to keep his money in place, and he seemed to know what he had in there to the penny. I carried everything, and we finally made our way back round to East Thomas Street. That area has totally changed now – all the old tenements have been replaced by new housing – but at that time it was still ramshackle and cobbled, making walking difficult for Blind Jimmy. I guessed that was why Helen had wanted me to help him. To be honest, I hadn't done much else. The old bloke could clearly cope with money and with dealing with people, so, apart from lugging his bags around, maybe I was there to make sure he didn't trip up or stumble.

Blind Jimmy lived in the type of area where 'hard life' was tattooed on every corner, on the face of every resident. Washing was either hung out in the unkempt front or back greens or from pulleys fixed to the outside of kitchen or bathroom windows in the upper apartments. So much for posh Edinburgh. Women sat nattering on doorsteps or across fences. Children ran around the streets yelling and screaming, playing hopscotch, kicking balls, skipping or scooting about on home-made carts. Hardly anyone had the luxury of a television or even a bike.

Blind Jimmy's flat was at the far end of the street on the ground floor. I helped him inside with his shopping and put it on a tatty table next to the cooker, the only space I could find. I was still waiting for him to engage me in conversation or even to recognise that I was helping out. The room he lived in was tiny and completely cluttered with junk. The bed was barely visible in a nook to the right of the door, and opposite was the cooking area. A sink was piled high with filthy dishes, and, apart from a small chair covered in clothes and paper bags, the only other bits of furniture were a table and sideboard. I couldn't wait to get out of there. The whole place was so dirty and depressing. 'Is there anything else I can help you with, Jimmy?' I asked. He turned slowly round, in the direction of my voice. He waited for a few moments, as if considering something, then wheezed, 'No. That's it.' As I went towards the door he called me back. 'Thanks. Thanks for helping. Here you go.' His gnarled, dirty hand held out a threepenny bit. I couldn't believe my luck! If I could hide it from Helen, spend it before I got home, then I could get something to eat. I took the money, left the flat, and ran to the shops as quickly as my legs would carry me.

❧

A few days later, Helen called me to her again. 'You can go and help Blind Jimmy,' she said, as if bestowing a great favour on me. 'Make him his dinner, you idle little bitch. Do something worthwhile for once. The poor old soul's not getting his meals-on-wheels today so he'll have to make do with you. Now, get moving, make him some mince and tatties – and don't show me up.'

I didn't like Blind Jimmy. He wasn't friendly. He was smelly and dirty and miserable, and his house was stinking and filthy too. After being in his house last time, I had scratched and itched for days. I hated being around him and I hated running Helen's errands, as I knew every time she sent me to 'help' someone, it made her look like a good person – and I didn't want any part of that. But, as usual, I couldn't disobey my stepmother's orders and I didn't really have any choice in the matter. The only glimmer of light was the thought of another threepenny bit if I was good. Well, I could do that, I could be good.

I made my way round to East Thomas Street. The sooner I got there, the sooner I could get this over with – and get some treats to eat. I knocked on the door and the old man answered it straight away. He was disgusting, dressed in shabby grey long johns which were full of holes. He had an old shirt on top of them, and I could smell him as soon as he opened the door. 'It's me, Jimmy,' I said. 'Wee Donna Ford? Helen says I've to make you some dinner? Mince and tatties?' Everything I said was phrased as a question to him, in the hope of getting a response. His swivelling, rheumy, unseeing eyes wandered about, then he turned, coughing, spluttering, and stumbled back into the flat without a word, climbing into his manky bed. I followed him in – it clearly wasn't going to be a chatty lunchtime, but that was fine by me. Maybe I could get done, get my money and get out even more quickly than I had first hoped. I looked over towards where the old man lay. The sheets looked as if they had never seen a bit of soap, and he was the same colour. Everything was grey, everything smelled. Maybe Helen did have a bit of good in her if she was willing to help some dirty old misery guts like this – even if it was actually me doing all the hard work.

I set myself to peeling and cooking potatoes, and heating up some mince that was already in a pot on the stove. There weren't any clean dishes – there wasn't anything clean in that place – so I washed a plate and a spoon and handed the meal over to Blind Jimmy, who still hadn't said a word to me. He ate the meal with all his usual spits and splutters – I concentrated on cleaning some more dishes to avoid listening to the sounds coming from him. Finally he had finished, and I had cleared up. I had only one thing on my mind – my threepence! Give me my threepence!

'Lassie! Come over here!' he finally called to me. I was so relieved. He hadn't forgotten why I was there. I went over to his bed, but instead of reaching for his grey hankie with the money in it, Blind Jimmy grabbed my hand. I screamed, both with the shock and also in disgust at him actually touching me. 'Let me go!' I shouted. His eyes were wavering all over the place, and his mouth was twisted into a toothless grin. He was small and he was old, but he had a grip of my right wrist and no intention of letting it go. I tried to pull away from him – pulling, pulling – but he pulled me harder. I fell onto the side of the bed, and as he pulled at me more, I found myself lying across his wizened, stinking old body.

I can still remember looking at the greyness – the sheets, his long johns, everything grey, everything hopeless. This pathetic old man, so often the butt of other people's jokes and cruelties, had found someone even weaker, even more pathetic. He pulled up my dress and whacked me across my backside. I tried to get up but he was holding me down, and, despite his frailty, his strength was greater than mine.

He was talking to me now. I could hear the words come closer to me. They sounded as if they were starting very far away, but the whispering got louder, the hissing got nearer – 'Shut up keep quiet shut up keep quiet shut up keep quiet.' I knew the drill. I was always to shut up. I was always to keep quiet. I couldn't help but cry – this was too much even for me. The smell, the disgusting old man touching me in places he shouldn't. 'Shut up. Keep quiet.' Self-preservation kicked in. He may have been old. He may have been blind. But he could still hurt me. I was so scared of what I knew he was going to do – and even more scared of what he might do if I kept making a fuss.

'Are you going to keep making that bloody racket?' he asked. He told me to stand up, even though he was still holding my hand. 'I can't. You're holding my hand too tight,' I protested. 'You bloody can and you bloody will,' he replied. 'I'm going to keep holding your hand and you're going to bloody well stand up, you little whore.' I stumbled to my feet awkwardly, with him still holding me as he moved my hand towards his penis. Fumbling around, he put his other hand inside my knickers. Standing there, totally humiliated, totally powerless, I watched myself being doubly abused by this pathetic old man. He masturbated himself with my hand as he fiddled around with me. Finally, he was finished. Finally, he let me go. My legs were trembling and I was sobbing. I was hurting. I was so embarrassed I couldn't think straight. I pulled my clothes together, wiped his filth off me, and headed for the door.

'Wee Donna Ford,' he shouted out after me. 'You'll keep quiet about this. You'll not breathe a word to a soul. You'll go home and you won't talk about it because no one would believe you, and the only person who would sent you here anyway.'

I ran out of his horrible, dark, smelly hovel and through the streets. I stopped only once – to vomit in a privet hedge on Elgin Terrace. As I threw up, I could hear children laughing and squealing in the playground next to the bowling green. I wasn't allowed out to play – but I was allowed out for this.

It had happened again. Just like all of those men who used me at Helen's parties. Just like all of the times Helen got me out of bed to 'do' something for one of her friends. Just like with the Barber. Just like it was with anyone who chose to use and abuse me. It had to stop. What Blind Jimmy had done to me had to be the last time.

I should have known better.

It happened three more times in that soiled hell hole with a pervert who had finally found someone weaker than himself. Each time I went because Helen told me to and because I was more scared of her than of anything else in the world. And I wasn't the only person who knew this – she did too, and that was much, much worse.

Chapter Thirteen

࿇

HELEN'S DEPARTURE
1970

THE VISITS TO BLIND JIMMY and the Barber stopped but there were always other men to take their place. The parties continued. My fear of the doorbell, my days of starvation and my whole miserable life went on as it had done since I was a little girl.

Until one day.

The day Helen left.

I knew that she and my Dad had been arguing even more than usual. Every little thing set her off, especially if it reminded her of my mother, the perpetual enemy. Once when my Dad was singing 'Danny Boy', Helen launched into a screaming session. 'There you go again!' she yelled. 'With your bloody Irish songs, always bringing *her* into it, always dragging *her* into things!' There had been continual shouting and screaming for some time. I had heard snatches of it but the noise and the atmosphere was such a constant in my life that I didn't pay too much attention. Helen always put my Dad down, always complained that he was at work and that they had no money. He couldn't win. As a child, I didn't understand it – surely if he didn't work as much, we would have even less money? On top of that, if he wasn't at work during the day, how could she continue with her parties? Perhaps she was calling his bluff – or perhaps, as I always hoped, he suspected she was up to something and that was the root cause of their fighting.

Whatever the reason, the outcome was all I had been wishing for since I was years younger. In the New Year of 1969/1970, Helen packed her bags and walked out of my life.

She left a legacy.

Not the bruises I still had all over my body. Not my broken dreams and waking nightmares. Not even the yearning I still had for a real Mummy.

She left Karen.

She was 18 months old when her mother deserted her – as Breda had deserted me – and I loved her with all my heart. When we had all lived together, I did have some interaction with Karen. As a baby, she bothered Helen, so I was often 'allowed' to walk her pram up and down the lobby, with the strict instructions that I was responsible for keeping her quiet and out of Helen's way. If I failed in my task, I knew what was coming to me. The natural cries or whimpers of a baby would result in another battering for me. So Karen and I walked many miles up and down that hallway, and I was already fond of her, even though we had minimal contact. I loved watching her chubby little face in her pram, and I always hoped I might be allowed to bathe her again after holding her once as she was splashing and giggling and Helen got on with something else. In the back of my mind was a worry that she might turn out like Gordon or Andrew, who had gone from innocent babies to nasty little sods given the teaching of their mother, but Helen seemed uninterested in her daughter, which gave me some hope.

How her mother could have left her is beyond me. When Helen left, I had to face up to so many emotions, a lot of them linked to Karen. Of course, I was ecstatic that my tormentor had gone, but her departure brought back feelings about my own mother leaving. Karen and I were in the same boat, really.

The morning after Helen walked out of the door, my life

changed yet again. I walked through to the kitchen where my Dad sat. He had been up all night, and was clearly upset. I felt a difference already. I wasn't scared. I didn't have a knot in my stomach. I could even ask a question without feeling the rings on her hand belting my face.

'Where is she, Dad?' I asked. 'Where's Helen?'

He looked up from the kitchen table where he had been staring, wordlessly. He looked so tired, so drained.

I heard the words I wanted to hear so badly.

'She's gone. And she won't be coming back.'

'Really? Truly?'

'Aye. I can promise you that you won't be seeing her again.'

I didn't know whether to believe him. However, the only promises I had been given in the past had actually come true, so maybe I could cling on to this one. Helen had been fond of saying I'd get a beating I'd remember – that she could promise me. I'd get walloped so hard I wouldn't be able to feel my legs – that she could promise me. If I said a word, I'd pay for it – that she could promise me. And she always kept her promises. Every time.

So maybe I could believe my Dad. Maybe she was gone. For ever.

I looked round. 'Who's still here, Dad? Who did she take with her?'

My Dad looked confused. And old.

'What?' he said, obviously not understanding what I was asking.

'Gordon? Andrew? Karen? Did she take them all? Where are they?'

'They're here. They're in bed. They're all here.'

She'd gone – but she'd left all of her children. Even precious Gordon. Part of me was terrified that she would be back, if only to collect him, but I should have realised that, as always, she was only interested in herself. I should also have known that mums can leave – they can leave three of their children quite easily and never be seen again. After all, Breda had done the same thing.

'What are we going to do now then, Dad?' I asked. I needed some guidance, some adult input – I wanted my Dad to show that, finally, he was going to do what was needed and be the sort of parent to keep this family together in the way it should be. He looked at me as if I'd just asked him to explain the theory of relativity. Then, his face changed – suddenly, he'd worked something out.

'What're we going to do?' he laughed. 'That's obvious, Donna. It's up to you. It's all up to you. You're the woman of the house now – you're in charge.'

I was 11 years old.

I had spent the past six years being beaten, starved and abused.

Now, all of a sudden, I was in charge. That was it. I was elated by Helen's absence but quickly realised there was still no time to be a child. Still no chance to be carefree and safe. I had gone from being nothing to being everything.

'And that bairn,' he said, referring to Karen. 'She's without a mother now, Donna – you'll have to be that for her. Best start now – best go through and see what she needs.'

I followed his instructions and went through to the cot where Karen slept. My heart was bursting and my brain was pounding. Helen was gone. I was in charge. Karen was standing up with her terry towelling nappy sagging around her knees. God knows how long it had been since she was last changed. It wouldn't have killed my Dad to see to her – he must have changed nappies when he first looked after the three of us when Breda left – but he obviously hadn't given it a second's thought last night. The poor little thing was drenched and stinking, but she still managed a great big smile for me. I struggled to lift her out of the cot, and finally hauled her over the side where I set about changing and dressing her. She was mine now, and I would do my best for her. Still, I was terrified. Helen could come back any minute – she'd catch me out of my room, catch me doing things she hadn't authorised, and I'd be beaten to within an inch of my life. I felt like that for a long time, even when it became obvious she wasn't in a hurry to return.

Over the next few days, my father made it clear that he meant what he'd said. I felt pleased. There was a nicer atmosphere than there had been in a long time, and I was chatting to my Dad on an equal basis. He had to rely on me and confide in me, and that felt good. I felt useful and needed. Helen wasn't coming back and it was all to rest on my skinny little shoulders. I was responsible for cooking, cleaning and keeping all the other kids in line. I had to beg money off my father for food, do the shopping and get the meals ready. I had to wait for him outside pubs, plead with him for a few pennies inside pubs. I had to make sure we had clothes and shoes and were washed and dried. Of course, it couldn't all be done, but I did my best. I was a little housewife, a little mother, within days.

It was hard work. Although Simon was older than me, he didn't have the same responsibilities as the girl, as the little woman. It was expected that I would carry everything, that I would be the one to keep the family together, no matter what. Karen took up so much of my time that, if I hadn't been so fond of her, it would have been unbearable. As it was, even little things like washing the nappies could take me all day. I was so little myself, so skinny and weak from years of neglect and malnutrition, that hard physical graft really took its toll. We didn't have a washing machine, so the soiled nappies had to be scraped, washed, steeped in a bucket, bleached, then washed again before being hung up to dry. In between times, I'd spend hours rushing in and out saving them from the rain, hanging them up again for a few minutes of sunshine, all day long. My arms ached. My back ached. It was work that would challenge a grown woman, never mind a scrap of a child. Karen was a happy baby though, and was seemingly oblivious to the chaos around her.

It was such a strange time for me as I had gone from being a prisoner, locked up most of the time, to a child with complete freedom in some ways. I could go where I wanted when I wanted – as long as I took Karen with me, had the meals ready for the rest of the family, and looked after the house. Some freedom for a child not yet in her teens, but a wonderful change for me. Some of the freedoms of the new role I had taken on, or been forced into, came at a price, however.

I became ill quite soon after Helen left. One morning I woke up in absolute agony.

'Dad!' I screamed. 'Dad! Help me!'

He rushed through to my tiny room to find me doubled up in pain.

'What's wrong, Donna? What have you done?'

I hadn't done anything! I was aching, but I still managed to notice that he put the blame on me before anything else. The pain was excruciating and it didn't go away, but it was made clear that I just had to get on with things. This continued for some days, with me screaming for him every morning and him eventually dismissing my cries.

Finally, it became too much to ignore and I was taken to the Royal Hospital for Sick Children. At the Sick Kids, I was given an immediate diagnosis. Appendicitis. My time in hospital was quite pleasant – I knew I was safe, and I had some respite from the constant cleaning and caretaking I had done since Helen left. My appendix was taken out and I soon returned home. However, the pains continued and I was being sick all the time. What was wrong with me? The doctors had done all they could and yet I was as ill as ever. Finally, I worked it out. I worked out what the doctors and my father had been blind to – presumably because they didn't see the full picture, they didn't ask the right questions or hear what they really needed to hear.

I was making myself ill with food.

When Helen left, my immediate thought was of food. I had

been hungry for so long that I had almost forgotten any other state. When she walked out, things went from one extreme to the other. For the first few months after she went, I ate anything, anything at all. I had gone from constant starvation to stuffing my face with whatever I could get hold of. And my body couldn't cope.

༚

I spent that whole summer looking after Karen constantly, without even school to break my days. And I loved every minute of it. That child continued to be a joy and a revelation to me. She was so happy, so perfect – and she loved me unconditionally. She seemed to have no memory of her mother as she certainly never cried for her or asked for her. I was the centre of her world and it felt wonderful. I remember taking her to a playgroup which was being held at a local school for the summer weeks while kids were on holiday. Both of us got a first chance to do things there which were completely alien to our lives before Helen left – arts and crafts, drama, rounders, even day trips to Edinburgh Zoo – all things other children may take for granted, but which I knew were daily miracles after the life I had been leading. I also loved the fact that I was the one responsible for giving Karen these experiences, this normality. She couldn't help being Helen's child, and she carried no badness in her from what I could see – I would make it my job to keep her free from any taint of evil which her mother might have bequeathed her.

Where I went, Karen went.

I am in no doubt that I saved myself from the scars of my childhood. No one else did that for me. But what Karen achieved for me was marvellous – she showed me not only that I could love, but also that I could be loved. The twisted irony was that it had taken the child of the woman who had wrecked my childhood to give that back to me.

᠅

Even in a miserable life such as mine, not everything was darkness. There has to be some relief from the unremitting cruelty for children like me. Sometimes it comes in the form of events, pets or new opportunities. For me, there were always people who brought some brightness, even if it was never enough. Where there had been Granny Ford and Auntie Nellie, and little Karen, there came another. He was Dr Ritchie to me and he was my science teacher at Norton Park School. I had started at High School in the August following Helen's departure.

James – or Jim – Ritchie is now quite well-known in Edinburgh circles. As well as being a teacher, he also had a huge interest in the games and rhymes of the capital's playgrounds. Dr Ritchie spent his working life of over 30 years as a maths and science teacher, but his spare time was dedicated to the real interests of the children he inspired. My old teacher discovered very quickly that, despite his talent for getting the best out of virtually every pupil he was allocated, nothing excited them more than play. He then made it his life's work to collect these games and songs and paraphernalia of play, both to engage and to record. His first collection of material formed the basis of a programme called *The Singing Street*, which was broadcast by the Scottish Home Service in 1949. This started a parallel career as a radio writer, and Dr Ritchie began his collation of Edinburgh children's history in earnest. He published two books on the subject in 1964 and 1965, and made a documentary which is still shown to this day in Edinburgh's Museum of Childhood.

James Ritchie was an incredibly kind man. By the time I reached Norton Park, I had suffered years of abuse and degradation. I didn't trust teachers – none of them had ever done anything for me in the past, and they all seemed to walk around with their eyes closed – but this one was different. I was still a tiny scrap of a thing, all bones and worry, but each time I had a science class with James Ritchie, he made me feel as if I was so important, the centre of the world at the moment he spoke to me. Science didn't draw me in – I was becoming more and more inclined towards art – but each time I entered the school lab, this gentle man would swing me up under my shoulders and lift me on to one of the workbenches so that I could see whatever experiment we were performing that day. 'There we go, wee Donna,' he'd say. 'Now you can see it all.' Sometimes he would sing to me, a German song, 'Donna Clara'. The Bunsen burners, the test tubes, the great big blackboard meant nothing to me educationally, but as parts of Dr Ritchie's world, they mattered. Every time he lifted me up, every time he spoke kindly to me, I got a glimpse of a life that could have been so different. Men could be nice. Men could be caring. They didn't always rape or abuse or hurt. There were men like James Ritchie in the world, and thank God for them.

Dr Ritchie was always interested if I had a rhyme to tell him, or a game to explain. He made me think that these things were important too. Looking back at the work he has left as his mark on history, I can see that he must have made many children feel this way. His books are full of the joys of childhood, the innocent pleasures children enjoy when they are left alone to play and sing. These were, of course, pleasures I rarely experienced, and, as an adult, reading James Ritchie's work is very poignant for me. I do feel bitter about the many adults, the many teachers, the many officials, who ignored – or simply never saw – what was happening to me as a child. However, I don't feel that way about Dr Ritchie because he truly did make me feel special, even if only for a few moments a week. Watching his film of *The Singing Street* brings different feelings. My memories of the man and his work had always felt good; there was nothing dark or wrong about how he was with me.

But a few years ago I discovered something that made me think twice – about fate and about the links which bind us all, even in ignorance. I was told that Helen Ford was one of the little girls in that film. She was one of the children playing innocently, singing and skipping. Happy. Untainted. I don't know which one she was. I don't know what her life was like then or how her life was in the subsequent years, years that made her into what she became. The coincidence strikes me to the very heart. The man who was one of the few kind people I ever encountered had brushed past the evil woman who ruined my childhood when she herself was so young. He had filmed her. He had, presumably, listened to her stories and her rhymes. And then, years later, he had lifted that child's stepdaughter up to his eye-level and made her feel good, normal and cared for – and he could never have known the bond between the two.

❧

There is a strong connection between the time I started High School and the time Helen left. Although many months separate the two, they both marked such clear 'coming of age' moments for me that they seem close. I was so happy that she had left and that I had some responsibility so the move to High School appeared as confirmation of my new status. I was caring for Karen – and doing a good job. Gordon couldn't intimidate me as much because I had some power in the household. Now, with High School looming, I could perhaps find myself.

Secondary school wasn't the new start I had hoped for. I can't remember any time when I was helped or encouraged with my homework, but I do remember going over and over my reading book and practising until I got it right. I loved being chosen to read aloud and spell. School was bittersweet. I wanted to excel and tried to, but I know now that the odds were stacked against me from the start. At least I could do some things, such as keep myself cleaner, but I was still not really part of any crowd. I was disillusioned but keen to try and do my best at something. I was the smallest in the class by far and felt really conspicuous. Although Helen had left the previous New Year and I'd had eight months without her influence, other pressures had taken her place.

It was noisy and busy at secondary school and there was lots of movement compared to primary. Bells were ringing all the time and people were constantly going from class to class. We were given a timetable on our first day – maths, English, history, domestic science, science, secretarial studies, art, PE, geography, fabric and fashion, French – all split up into single, double or, at times, treble periods. I loathed secretarial studies – it was boring beyond belief – Pitman's shorthand and learning to type as fast as you could without looking. It seemed stupid and senseless, given that I didn't ever want to be a secretary.

However, I did discover where my real interest lay – in art. When Norton Park and Leith Academy amalgamated, I was moved to the main school at the bottom of Easter Road. This was a different scene altogether. The 'rector' of the school, Mr McKay, was an ex-rugby player so rugby played a big part in the school curriculum. It was a sporty school in every sense. Hockey, which I hated because it involved being even colder than usual and hurt a lot, seemed to be always on the agenda. But the art department was wonderful. I relished those sessions. Even though I skived off school frequently, I always tried to get to my art classes, and even swapped with someone from my registration class – my secretarial sessions for their art. Nothing was ever said. I loved it so much – it freed me and challenged me.

Sadly, apart from Dr Ritchie and the art classes, I have few good memories of Norton Park. My chores and responsibilities didn't make me stronger – just exhausted. Every morning, I got up before the rest of the family to make sure the house was clean. Then I had to get everyone else up and make sure they all had breakfast. Once Karen was clean and changed, I set off for her nursery. It was some distance away, on Newhaven Road, and I rarely had the money for the bus fare. This meant that each day before school, I would have walked from my house to Karen's nursery and then from her nursery to school. I was always tired, and usually late.

I was still skinny and scrawny, and I never felt this more than when I was at High School. From the first day onwards, I felt out of place. I suffered from styes and had a big chip on my front tooth. I wore a second-hand school uniform that was far too big for me. I was so thin that I wore three pairs of tights to try and make my legs look fatter. The whole experience was always intimidating, and teachers – apart from Dr Ritchie – didn't make it any better.

I would much rather have been home looking after Karen. Instead I had to face the wrath of one teacher after another. They saw a skinny, uncared-for, smelly kid who was always tired and rarely engaged with anything other than art. Just as it had been at junior school, they looked no further than the surface. Miss Mutch was our headmistress, a stern, grey-haired woman who never smiled, and she typified the whole school.

Sometimes an incident would remind me sharply of what I had lived through. There was one English teacher called Mr Robertson, nicknamed 'Penguin' because of the way he walked. He was a quiet man, not very tall, and balding. One day he was having trouble controlling some boys in his class who were playing up whenever his back was turned. Something had been thrown when Penguin's back was turned and nobody would own up. He'd had enough and declared that everyone was to get two of the belt. As he got out his large, strong leather tawse, I stared shaking. Beatings had been so much a part of my life but I hadn't been hit since Helen left. I don't know how I got through such a traumatic event, but it served as a reminder that the past would always be there, threatening to rise up at any moment.

I was also terrified by the school playground. I didn't have any friends so felt completely alone at break and lunchtimes. I spent most of my time hiding away as, yet again, I didn't fit in. My favourite hiding place was the girls' toilet – the memory of the powdered soap and green crispy hand towels is still strong. I would spend ages running my hands under the hot tap trying to warm them as I was always cold.

As well as the cold, I always felt tired. The drudgery of my life was draining me completely. I rarely had time to play, or do any of the childish things I had dreamed of, even now Helen was gone. I often fell asleep in class only to be woken by the sound of a teacher's belt or ruler on the table in front of me. Eventually I ended up only going to school for the art lessons. Nothing else mattered, nothing else touched me, so I truanted most of the time.

I was putting parts of me away – and that might be the only way I could cope.

Chapter Fourteen

∾

MOVING ON ...

1973–1976

HELEN MAY HAVE BEEN physically out of my life for a few years, but the residue of her impact was still there. I had spent so much of my life doing little more than surviving that I didn't really have the building blocks all young people deserve, the foundations which would help me on the next stage of my life. Even as a teenager, I had few friends. It was hard for me to trust people; it was hard even to know what to say to them when they asked questions about me. Should I rewrite my past, or just try to evade any investigations, no matter how friendly, when they arose?

From around the age of 14, I started going out to the local youth club, which was held in a church on Easter Road. Even the concept of going out whenever I wanted, to places I chose, was still foreign to me. The youth club itself was probably pretty grotty, but to me it was full of opportunities. Attending the club finally gave me the chance to make some friends and do normal, childhood things which had been denied to me in my life with Helen.

In general we'd all meet up in the church hall and hang out there, playing pool, listening to music. It was just mucking about really, but the innocence of it all seemed like a gift to me. I was completely accepted because no one at the youth club knew anything about my home life or what had happened there. This was hard for me to come to terms with – I actually thought I was so transparent that people could see my shame. As a child, while the abuse was ongoing, it had eventually dawned on me that it was all hidden, it was all secret. Nobody knew. However, as I got older, my thoughts swung the opposite way, and I found it remarkable that people couldn't tell just by looking at me what a horrible, shameful girl I was. Wasn't it obvious? Couldn't they work it out? When I finally started to believe that they couldn't see, they couldn't tell, I really began to look forward to the weekly youth club evening.

The organiser also took us all on trips. I was allowed to go on three of them. As well as the friendship and fun that coloured each occasion, I also began to learn things about myself. One trip was for the day to Yellowcraigs beach; the second was a full weekend break to a barn near Eddleston in Peeblesshire; and the final trip was four days spent on Iona. These were magical places to me, and each of them showed me just how much nature meant to my developing senses, how peaceful and settled I could feel in the right environment. But the trips didn't come easily. I remember one of the youth leaders coming round to the house in an attempt to persuade my Dad that I should be allowed to go on the Eddleston trip. My Dad was very reluctant. He tried to get out of it by saying he couldn't afford the cost – naturally a lie since he always had enough for booze – but the youth leader called his bluff by saying she'd pay my contribution. Dad still clung to as many excuses as he could muster – I was too young, I was too irresponsible, I wouldn't enjoy myself. Obviously, none of this was true. He admitted, once the youth club woman had left, that he just couldn't run the house without me. Again, his needs were to take priority. I don't remember what eventually caused him to change his mind – but luckily he did.

Eddleston was such a memorable weekend. We stayed in some old farm buildings, surrounded by fields. We ate and socialised in a main building and slept in the loft of a barn, which was decked out with campbeds and sleeping bags for all the kids. The ghosts didn't all stay away – you take your baggage with you even on holiday – but I managed at least to cope with my fear of night-time, the dark and the shadows, all of which had stayed with me since my time in the cellar in Easter Road. We all went on walks through woods and fields; we ate around a big table together; and, in the evenings, the youth leaders (who were all quite young themselves) played guitars and sang around the fire. It was magical for me. Every time I hear 'A Whiter Shade of Pale' it reminds me of that time and brings a smile to my face.

The trip to Iona was, however, the most magical of my childhood years. Although there were many other children there that I didn't know, I had never felt so peaceful. Even the journey there was fascinating. We got the coach to Oban, followed by a ferry to Mull, and then finally a little boat that took us over to Iona itself. Even now when I think about it, I can still feel the bubbles of excitement churning in my stomach. Iona is beautiful with ancient buildings and history, and a landscape to make you think there is no better place in the world. Although Iona is so small that you can walk around it in next to no time, it also feels as if all the world is contained in that one little island. It was just what I needed – the feeling of being part of something much bigger, and of feeling safe on my terms really helped me.

All these experiences helped to open my mind to a world away from Easter Road. They confirmed what I knew, what I had to believe in – someday I'd get away.

～

Like every other place in Britain during the 1970s, Edinburgh in general – and Easter Road in particular – had its own gangs. This didn't necessarily mean anything sinister, especially not for a young girl. However, there were specific, yet unwritten, rules which made it quite clear that the music you liked determined how you dressed, how you acted, and even who your mates could be.

I did have two 'friends' in my adolescent years. Neither of them went to the same school as me, but they did live locally and we had formed some sort of bond when playing in the 'street' (which, in itself, was still a novelty to me). These girls weren't friends in the sense of being great pals with whom I could share every secret, every thought. They were really just people I hung out with. We were in the same place at the same time – but they were still the nearest I had. I remember two main things about them – their family life and the strict fashion codes they adhered to. If I ever managed to get anywhere close to a best friend, it was Joan MacKenzie. She was from a family of five girls and one boy who lived nearby, and they made such a difference to me. Joan was the youngest of the family; they all called her 'Tootie'. I still had a problem working out why anyone would be nice to me without asking for something in return, but the MacKenzies always tried so hard. They would give me their cast-off clothes, ask me round for tea, and even include me in their Christmas parties. I've always wondered whether they suspected any of what I had been through, or whether they were just basically good people who helped those around them without question. They were such a loving family, and even though they didn't have much, they shared with me and with others. This was another world to me – I had rarely seen generosity or kindness for its own sake before, and although it warmed me to the core, it also made me utterly ashamed of my home life.

Joan didn't go to the same school as me, but two of her elder sisters did, which was the only way I was able to get a school uniform for Leith Academy. We weren't drawn to each other because of our similarities at all. Joan was really popular as she was very confident. She was so different to me, and so was her home life, yet we did get along well. We'd hang around together whenever I could get time away from my chores. What I remember really clearly about her is that she always knew exactly what to wear, exactly how to look so that she could fit in. She knew the rules, and everything about her just seemed effortless.

Joan had long light-brown hair, in contrast to my short dark crop. I was trying to hide, make myself invisible to anyone who might be inclined to show an interest in me, but Joan didn't have to worry – her solid, happy home life meant she could have a solid, happy adolescence too.

Music was really important to all of us. Joan was Donny Osmond mad. She'd play his album over and over, and spoke about him all the time. Teenage pop star obsession is fickle, and although we were all sure we would absolutely die for love, it didn't take much more than a new face on the scene to convince us that things needed to change. I took my cue from Joan. Donny and the rest of the Osmonds were soon ousted when the Bay City Rollers arrived. Not only did they seem impossibly gorgeous to us, they were from Edinburgh too! Joan got all their records and was even allowed to dress like them, with extra bits of tartan added to the bottom of her cropped trousers. Tootie was always more fashionable, more popular and much happier than I was. I felt so dull next to her, but I also felt that was what I deserved.

ॐ

The other friend I had at that time was Sandra Dunlop. Sandra was also a different type of person from me entirely. She seemed so much more mature than me. Even though I had been through unthinkable things from such a young age, it didn't make me precocious or mature for my years. Instead, I looked to these other girls for clues as to how should I act. What would look normal? Joan and Sandra gave off very different messages.

Sandra's family felt different to Joan's. Sandra had more freedom of an adult sort, in that she went to parties and had a harder confidence to that of Tootie, but I didn't envy her in the same way. Sandra lived in Easter Road too. Her first-floor flat was the cleanest place I had ever seen. At that time, I used to marvel at how house-proud her mother was – she'd get up at the crack of dawn every day and start to scrub. Mrs Dunlop didn't put down her duster, her bleach, her scrubbing brush or her vinegar until she went to bed. Sandra's father had some connection with the whaling industry, which wasn't unusual in that part of Edinburgh at the time, and Mrs Dunlop was always fussing about all the pieces of carved whalebone on their mantelpiece. In those days, all that struck me as remarkable was the fact that I got lamb chops when I once went for my tea. Lamb chops! It was like another world.

Our definition of 'party' may seem a bit pathetic – some of us going round to someone else's house and sitting about – but these get-togethers were infinitely better than anything I associated with the word when Helen was in my life. Sandra would arrange for four or five of us to go over to a boy's house while his parents were out. We'd listen to David Bowie's *Spiders from Mars* album over and over, and all share a bottle of cheap Pomagne. Quite the high life when you're 15! Once or twice a boy called Graham Forrest would be there, and he was really the only one I ever had any 'action' with at the time. Graham and I would snog and he'd 'try it on', but frankly I was so petrified of any intimate contact that I'd spurn him as soon as he started. At one point he got really annoyed with me, jumped up from the sofa, and informed the entire room that I was 'tighter than a duck's arse'. I could deal with it. I'd dealt with worse. If people wanted to see me as a virginal type who barely knew how to deal with boys, that was preferable to them knowing the truth or even uncovering my terror of them.

One day, Sandra wasn't around. I didn't bother to ask where she was as we all came and went without any promises to each other. But, as the days stretched into weeks, Sandra's absence became more and more marked. Eventually, someone told me she had gone to live with her Auntie. Now, that was one of the great euphemisms of our day. 'Going to live with your Auntie' could mean only one thing – Sandra was pregnant.

Nothing had changed much since my mother's time. Fifteen-year-old girls like Sandra could still be playing hopscotch in the street one day, and then whisked off to an anonymous family member with their bellies full the next. Despite having her marked down as a general 'friend', Sandra and I hadn't really spoken of anything important. I didn't even know she'd been having sex. I'm not sure whether the gravity of the girl's situation hit me at that time. Pregnant, unmarried teenagers were still considered bad girls, with little said about the men who had got them into that condition. Even with my own experiences, I had no idea what Sandra's story was.

I knew what was all around me. I had lived it. And yet the community was still incredibly prudish and judgemental. Within parochial areas like Easter Road, men seemed to get off scot-free. It was the girls and the women who carried the shame and the guilt; they were the ones who were called names and whose families disowned them. It never ceased to amaze me that this charade continued so effectively. I sometimes felt as though all the grown-ups must have sat down together and worked out a plan. If that had happened, what were women getting out of it? There was still an over-riding notion that women should 'save' themselves for marriage, and yet men were allowed – encouraged – to sow their wild oats and be one of the lads. When Sandra arrived back from her Auntie's with a baby boy in tow, she was the only one who had to face up to the consequences, the whispers behind her back, and the harsh appraisals of the women who seemed to put so much energy and vitriol into keeping other women in their 'place'.

Looking at Sandra with a baby at 15, and seeing how hard she was working, made me swear I would never be in her shoes. I would live some before I brought new life into this world, and I'd find myself before finding a baby at my side. Although there were teenage hormones all around me, to some extent I was safe. No one had ever had the slightest idea about my abuse while it was going on, which meant that, in the little world of those around, I was a 'good girl'. I did have one or two boyfriends in my early teenage years, but I felt so soiled by what had been done to me that I probably had much less experience with them than other girls my age. I always felt that they would know what had gone on in my past if we ever got to a sexual relationship, so I avoided that sort of development at all costs.

I took what lessons I could from my relationship with these girlfriends. From Joan's family, there was such basic goodness; from Sandra, a warning that things were still very different for girls and hypocritical. Put together with what Auntie Nellie had given me, I looked forward. I really, really wanted to leave Edina Place. Despite everything that had happened to me, I could build on the good parts of life I had glimpsed – I truly felt I could achieve something. Mostly, books had taught me that there was a very different world out there. I just had to go and find it.

I harboured wild dreams at that time of becoming a famous artist and returning to Edinburgh in splendour, to show that I was something or somebody. If it didn't quite happen like that, it would be enough for me just to say: 'You didn't keep me here. I got away.' I didn't want to stay in that tiny little world, and just end up with someone for the sake of it. I needed to avoid that, to avoid falling into a relationship which would simply perpetuate my unhappiness and prevent me from finding out who I really was. I had to get away from what I saw as my prison.

᷒

When I look back on the time I left the family home to set out on my adult path, I am shocked by just how naïve and unprepared I was. I'd had so many experiences and seen so many things a child should never go through, yet I was lacking in many vital skills that any young person needs when they are starting out. The list was endless. I didn't have any basic social skills at all. I didn't know how to form relationships. Amazingly, I was undeterred. It's only now that I realise what I didn't have and what I didn't know. Back then, I just went for it. I didn't feel at all sad or sorry for myself; instead I was filled with a quiet excitement about what was in store for me in my life. And the prospect that I was – finally – getting away.

At 17, I ended up almost 200 miles away in the Highlands of Scotland. In Inverness, I finally settled in a job as an auxiliary nurse at a rest and rehabilitation centre for geriatrics. I didn't have a particular penchant for this sort of work – I took it because it came with accommodation. At last, I had my own place, or the nearest I had ever come to it – a room in nurses' quarters on the top floor of the residence building alongside other hospital staff. There were quite a few young women my age living there, and although I did go out with them at times, I was never really that close to them. They all seemed to manage some easy bond, sitting in each other's rooms swapping clothes, make-up, stories about boys, tales about their families. They seemed different. They seemed normal. I wanted to be part of it all, but I spent a lot of time on my own through choice. I was too embarrassed to ask if I could join in. I'm sure, looking back, that if I'd asked to join in they would have been more than happy to let me, but I still had a fear of being let down or turned away when I tried to enter 'normal' worlds.

Instead, I bought a bike and would cycle anywhere and everywhere. It was the summer of 1976 and it was incredibly hot, giving me the chance to be outdoors most of the time. I made the most of my freedom, which was always what had mattered most to me, and I had other things that brought me such joy too. I loved dressing up, and would scour antique and charity shops for wonderful things to wrap myself in. I went on my own to local discos and pubs, knowing that the other nurses and auxiliaries tended to hang out there. I felt more confident that they would talk to me, include me, if I was there 'by chance' than if I had deliberately made myself vulnerable by asking to go along with them in the first place.

There was a sense of loneliness and not belonging, but I had at least achieved my main goal – I wasn't living back *there* any more. Surely now, I would be free of my past?

Chapter Fifteen

ॐ

... AND CATCHING UP

THE MOVE FROM EDINBURGH, the cutting of links, wasn't entirely successful. My past wasn't quite ready to let go of me.

Before I left for Inverness, I had been seeing a man called Martin. I wouldn't have said Martin was my boyfriend – but he was one of the first men I had an adult sexual relationship with. The rapes and abuses I suffered as a child never struck me as part of my sex life, not the one I had as a consenting adult. Sadly, compartmentalising life isn't quite that easy. Martin may not have been my boyfriend, and I may not have been that child of my past, but I still found myself in a situation where I felt I was being used for sex. The relationship I had with him is difficult to unpick now, even in retrospect, but I do know that I almost expected to be degraded and objectified. I still found it hard to believe that anyone could love me, that anyone could treat me with respect. I just thought bad relationships were what I deserved.

All this meant that Inverness was becoming an option I liked more and more. But there were other ties I had to deal with. I still wrote to my Dad and Karen, and sent some of my wages back, but my letters never received any replies. After six months in the job, I was ready for my first Christmas away from home.

Although I had never spent the festive period in a particularly traditional setting, even for me this was to be an especially empty time. Most people were fighting to get home, back to their families, but I chose to work through to stop myself thinking about the fact that, again, I didn't have all I really wanted.

Christmas morning for me wasn't quite what dreams are made of. I spent it cleaning out bedpans, changing beds and serving dinner to the residents before going off duty in the afternoon and heading back to empty staff quarters. I had forgotten to get myself any food in, and it had also slipped my mind that the staff canteen wouldn't be open that day. I ended up with some savoury rice quickly heated up, and a session in front of the telly watching *Charlie's Angels*. I have to admit that I did feel a bit sorry for myself that day. I didn't have a single card or letter or present from home. When all of the girls were showing off their gifts or talking about the traditions they were going home to, I felt embarrassed. Again. How could I talk about the memories of Christmas for me? Should I tell them about the empty 'Tiny Tears' box? Should I make them feel bad by informing them of how even the smells of Christmas cooking could take me back to days of starvation and torture? Any time they asked what I was getting or where my family was, I felt worse. It was becoming clearer and clearer to me that I couldn't rely on what was left of my family for anything. I had to fight the guilt I felt about leaving Karen behind and try to move forward myself.

❧

I can't explain exactly why, but I stayed in Inverness for only a year before moving back to Edinburgh. I had enjoyed my work in the geriatric home, but there was still too much unfinished business in Edinburgh, too many ghosts to lay to rest. I still enjoyed drawing whenever I could, but my dream of becoming an artist seemed out of reach. I knew I needed to concentrate on

getting a decent job, a recognised profession, to prevent me slip-
ping back into dependency. Being secure, being settled, was all I
wanted. Once I had that, perhaps I could look towards what my
heart really desired.

When I arrived back in Edinburgh, I got a job similar to that
in Inverness, as an auxiliary nurse in the City Hospital, again
living in nurses' quarters. One day I bumped into Martin again,
and before long had started back in a relationship with him.
Nothing had changed but I was so grateful that someone would
even consider taking on me, with all my baggage, that I accepted
it as part of the deal.

Before long, Martin had persuaded me to move out of the
residences at the City Hospital and to stay in a flat with him and
one of his friends. Going 'home' was again becoming something
to endure. Work was no better. From enjoying nursing and
planning to take it further as a career option, I was becoming
thoroughly disillusioned. The care of geriatrics at that point
wasn't just archaic – it was cruel. I could barely stand to be
around daily instances of people being treated so badly, so
inhumanely. Was this the end of the cycle which would wait for
me as I became old? Would I end as I had started? Was age – at
either end of the spectrum – simply an excuse for people to
debase others for their own convenience? Again, I saw the
hypocrisy and the charades that went on. Old people, who were
treated like dirt for the entire week, would be wheeled out,
infantilised and made to put on a show when their relatives
arrived for a 30-minute weekend visit. These people, who were
often quite deliberately left in their own shit and piss for hours
on end, were suddenly patronised for the benefit of other adults
who needed lies spun for them so that they could continue their
lives, unfettered, for the rest of the time. It was too familiar for
me to bear. I honestly felt that my conscience couldn't stand it a
moment longer. Again, my guilt kicked in. I knew that by
leaving, I couldn't possibly make their lives any better – but I had

to balance fighting a system with saving myself.

At that point, Martin knew someone who was working at a children's home in the Morningside area of the city. I'd been along there on a few occasions to run classes for some of the kids, where we would have whole afternoons painting and making things with craft materials. I absolutely loved it. I was never prouder than when I was helping those kids see what they could achieve artistically. When the home began recruiting new members of staff, the officer-in-charge suggested that I apply for a position. I had no idea where my life was going, and this seemed as good an avenue to wander down as any other. I was offered a post almost immediately, and my career in social work began.

Martin and I were continuing what I now know was a really unhappy relationship. I was so very needy because of what happened to me as a child, and had no other experience to go on. I didn't honestly know what other people expected or accepted in their private lives – all my experiences had been mucked up since the start, so what could I compare things with? If I had been blessed with the knowledge I have now, I wouldn't ever have gone out with Martin. However, as in my childhood, there were times when I could take something from what I was going through. I learned much more from the everyday world he introduced me to – the world which was perfectly normal to him. Martin's middle-class upbringing in a well-to-do area had given him an education which went way beyond school. He and his friends knew about life in ways I couldn't imagine. They knew how to talk freely, how not to be embarrassed by their accents or grammar, how to eat in restaurants without feeling ill or stupid, how to be just an average person. The time I spent in the company of Martin and his circle was of great value to me personally. I could soak up their conversation or even just wallow in the carefree fun they could enter into without even thinking. The more I saw of this, the more I wanted. The 1970s for me were a time when I was still trying to come to terms with my past and dealing with the fact that it still allowed me to suffer abusive personal relationships – but I was also just a teenager. I went to Led Zeppelin, The Who, and Alex Harvey concerts. I read *The Hobbit*, *Lord of the Rings*, and *The L-Shaped Room*. I joined in their discussions about Marxism, existentialism, and Communism. We carelessly discussed classical versus abstract art. Often I didn't have a clue what I was talking about, but I joined in anyway. I was part of it all.

The most important aspect of that time in my life was not just that I was free, but that I was being accepted as a person by people I felt were so much better than me. They never asked about my background, so I didn't have to lie or avoid the issue. Perhaps I was finally becoming someone I could be comfortable around, someone I could love. Yet while the real Donna was perhaps finally coming through, I was still haunted by thoughts of the past and the unanswered questions for the parent who should have answered them.

Chapter Sixteen

꩜

MY HERO

MY FATHER, DONALD CHALMERS FORD, was the first person I ever pinned any hopes on. I remember the Sunday visits from him at the Barnardo's home. He'd come with a rolled-up bundle of comics – *The Beano* and *The Dandy* for Simon, *Jackie* for Frances and *Twinkle* for me. Helen would be with him, but all I remember is her holding the baby – Gordon – and bouncing him on her knee. We'd all be brimming with happiness and chattering. Frances always sat beside him, and even though he was only my Dad, not theirs, he was the only father figure they knew, so we all looked to him for that support, that security. I was holding on to him for dear life the day we made the momentous journey home to Easter Road for good. I remember looking at him constantly and chattering, and he answered all my questions. So how did he become the man who allowed Helen to do what she did? As I've said before, she made her choices – as did all of her 'friends', as did all of the men who abused me – but my father wasn't innocent. As the only blood parent I knew, I had so many expectations pinned on him. He never really delivered, and I'm now left with such a mixed bag of memories that I hardly know what to think of him, the man who should have been my hero.

Everyone called him Don. He wasn't a tall man – about five foot seven. He wore a white shirt every day. When he was at home, his shirt sleeves would be rolled up, his tie off, and he'd have a sleeveless pullover or a cardigan on, the type with pockets in the front and big brown buttons. When he was going out, he'd take off the pullover and don his tie, suit jacket and winter overcoat. Being an ex-army man, his shoes were always polished. I know of the services part of his life only from seeing photos of him in Germany, posing with his comrades, and some of him swimming in a river having fun. He seemed to be acting like a different person in those pictures, but I was getting used to people having 'fronts', to having so many faces they put on, that I didn't necessarily see my Dad as someone who was living a life he had never anticipated. I knew that he had also trained as a French polisher because he was always doing something with bits of furniture, and he had boxes full of tools and endless bottles of lacquer and varnish. He loved to tell people about his 'skills', and he was quite a good carpenter too. I can remember when he'd be busy sanding and polishing odd bits of furniture for someone, and the smell of shellac still reminds me of those times.

There seemed to be such a contrast in the ways he behaved, according to whatever was going on at the time – and it was Helen who always determined the tone of family life. I did look up to him when I first arrived home; he was my Dad, and even at that age I knew what Dads were for. But Helen made it very clear to my Dad that I was nothing special, and I shouldn't expect anything. Gordon was her child – and he should take precedence over me, even in the early days. She had told me straight away that she was not my Mum and I was never to consider her as such. I was such a tiny little thing and so desperately in need of love that my desire for his attention actually hurt me. I had so many questions – why didn't he pick me up? Why didn't he sit me on his knee as he did with Gordon? Why did I never really get any notice taken of me unless it was bad? I just wanted to be cuddled, I just wanted to belong to a proper family; but Helen made sure it was never going to happen, and my Dad did absolutely nothing to stand in her way. We were both put in our places really.

I heard Helen shouting so much in those early days – it wouldn't stop as the years went on, but I wasn't used to it yet. She would tell him that I wasn't to be spoiled, that I was to be made to realise how lucky I was. It seemed to me that everything was very difficult, even though I had no idea why or what place I played in it all. My Dad rarely stood up to her – and if he did, it was only verbally and briefly before he left the house yet again. He seemed to be working all the time. When I first went there, he worked on the buses. When I was very young, he would arrive back from work on a Friday evening with his pay-packet in his pocket, which he gave to Helen immediately. Sometimes my Dad would have a comic for me, and always – every Friday evening – he brought a brand-new Matchbox car, still in its little cardboard box, for Gordon, his son with Helen. Dad was very affectionate with Gordon, picking him up and throwing him around play-fully. I can remember watching the scenes and envying Gordon his easy life. That child was never hit, never starved, never abused – in fact, it wouldn't be long before he would turn on me too.

I remember getting to go on the number one bus in Easter Road (the one Auntie Nellie and I had also taken). It was an old-fashioned double decker bus with no door, just a pole to hold on to, then upstairs, two wooden steps at a time. I'd hear him call: 'Tickets please!' Then he'd come around with his metal ticket box, turning the handle, issuing the pink ticket with the blue writing giving stage number and price, and with 'Edinburgh Corporation Buses' stamped on to it. I can remember him walking up the wooden slatted floor in his blue serge uniform with the metal and enamel badge clipped to his jacket. Everyone chatted and endured the bumpy ride up the cobbled street – they all cracked jokes and bantered with each other. I take it he didn't earn much on the buses, and it wasn't long before Helen started hassling him about their lack of money. He then took a job in the General Post Office in Edinburgh, while we still lived in Easter Road, which meant he left really early in the morning. My Dad took as many extra shifts as he could and just stopped ever really being around.

I remember his Post Office jacket hanging up on a peg, with its brass embossed buttons, alongside the old sack bag in which he carried the mail. On one very rare occasion, he took me to deliver letters with him. We were still living in Easter Road at the time. The beatings and punishments had already started and it was summer. I'd had a kicking from Helen while my Dad was standing in a corner of the tiny shared bedroom. I don't know who else was in the house but I could hear kids playing in the back green as usual. Don and Helen had been shouting at each other for what seemed like for ever and I knew what was coming. Helen had started blaming any of the disruptions in the house on me. I listened to them as they stood over me – it was all going to be laid at my door again. 'She's a little madam,' she was screaming. 'She's a spoilt brat.' It all just became noise after a while, but on this day there was a break to the pattern. Suddenly, I was told to get dressed by my Dad. We were going out. I couldn't believe my luck! Getting away from Helen was a treat in itself, but getting my Dad to myself was something so rare that I could hardly contain myself. Was he finally cottoning on to her? We went all the way to Wallyford on his bike, with me perched on the crossbar, and delivered a batch of letters. After my Dad had done his deliveries, he bought me a bun from Crawford's the bakers. I hardly remember the beating – that was becoming my normality – but I do recall the delight of being with my Dad, away from it all.

He was and still is a bit of an enigma to me. My feelings regarding him are so mixed that I don't know quite what to do with them. I know he beat me when I was a small child but I also know that it was at the insistence of Helen. When she left he gave me the odd 'cuff round the lug' but never beat me. My best memories of him are when he visited me in the Barnardo's home, because he was always smiling in those days and bearing gifts: sweets, magazines, a little toy. It's only when I moved back home that the memories become more contradictory. When Frances and Simon came back from Barnardo's, Dad would take us for walks if there was any time he wasn't working. I can remember him taking all of us on walks around Arthur's Seat, with a bag of boilings from Casey's at the top of Easter Road stuffed in his pocket to dole out when it looked like we were getting bored. He'd tell us all about Holyrood Palace and the park and we'd go and feed the swans at St Margaret's Loch. I also remember him taking us to Chambers Street Museum and to the Museum of Childhood. He took all of us there for years – including Karen when she was small enough to be in her pram. Helen was never there so they are fond memories. However, when all the arguments started between him and Helen, it suddenly seemed that he wasn't around much.

It's not easy to speak about the feelings I had – and have – for my father because he let me down so badly. He was the only one who could have really saved me, and he didn't. I don't know if he was controlled by Helen in the same way that I was, but what other answer can I hold on to? He did many things that said he was not a bad man. He knew that Helen's youngest child was not his, yet he reared her as his own after she left. Never do I recall him letting on to Karen that she wasn't his – he didn't call her names or stigmatise her or make her feel less like one of his own.

When Helen left us, I asked him why he would bring up a child who wasn't his own and who was a constant reminder of Helen. He just replied, 'It's no' the bairn's fault.' Karen always had a high regard for him, and I know that many of the people who knew my father really liked him. It was often said to us that he was a kind man. But from my perspective, I find it so hard to know what he was all about.

⌁

When Helen left, Dad's pub visits became even more frequent. He started going to Middleton's all the time, and it escalated from being 'a quick pint' or 'a wee bit of company' to the place being his second home. I hated that place and everything it stood for. After Helen had gone, I did have hopes of us being a real family in a proper home, not a permanently pissed-up excuse for a Dad in a stinking boozer rolling in at all hours. 'It's just a wee drink, hen,' he'd say. 'Just trying to enjoy mysel' a wee bit.' But, for me, men and drink and so-called enjoyment rarely meant fun or happiness. Even though I was still so young and faced with the responsibility of looking after Karen, I harboured such dreams. If only Dad would stay out of Middleton's, maybe our family could finally be put back together again.

My life settled into a new pattern. I'd still come tearing out of school, still have others waiting for me. But now, it was a race to get home, pick Karen up, stick her in her tatty buggy and push her up Easter Road to try and beg some money off Dad for our dinner. The pubs closed for a while in the afternoon, but by the time I got us going, he was back there, propping up the bar or slumped in a chair – I wouldn't have known where else to find my Dad. I always had high hopes of getting a pound each time, but it all depended on how much he'd drank, how guilty he felt about five children needing to be fed, and how lucid he was. I'd shove the door of Middleton's open with my backside as I reversed in with the buggy. The stench of stale beer, fag smoke and dead lives hit me like a brick wall. All the men looked the same. You couldn't really identify their ages; they were wrecked to the same stage. Perfect specimens of poor eating and good drinking, these men in their little worlds could see nothing wrong with a child having to beg money off her own father so that she could feed the baby she had been left with.

Apart from Middleton's, Dad liked the bowling club, the Hibs club, and the merchant seamen's club. All of these 'clubs' took food out of the bellies of children like me and Karen, and sent more drunk men home to families who needed the money – families who didn't need the sorry excuses for fathers and husbands who thought their need for 'a wee bit of company' was the be-all and end-all.

Still, there were worse things than my Dad being on his own in a pub, with me and Karen pathetically begging for his spare change. Worse by far were his 'mates'. By the time I was about 13 or 14, on quite a few occasions – too many – Dad would have someone 'staying over'. These great pals of his were generally just other lushes from the pub, who suddenly became a bosom buddy over another pint and a sob story. Sometimes he barely knew them; other times he'd been drinking with them for years but had still only scratched the surface of any so-called friendship forged through beer goggles.

I actually felt sorry for some of them, even the ones who would cadge off us for weeks on end, sleeping on the sofa in the living room. There was one man called Ernie who was absolutely fine. When Dad staggered home with him, amidst much backslapping and calls of camaraderie, I wasn't bothered. Ernie was genuinely down on his luck – he had suffered some accident at work and lost fingers through a chainsaw incident, I think. He would just doss down when he needed to, and not really bother any of us. He certainly never touched me or made me feel uncomfortable. There was another bloke whose name I can't remember, even though I can picture him really clearly. He was incredibly tall – to me – with sandy hair, and I recall him saying that he was in the Merchant Navy. He had an air of respectability about him,

and was, indeed, always very respectful to me, despite my youth
and the fact that my Dad didn't exactly set the scene for anyone
to treat me particularly well.

But there were others. There always had been.

დ

Dougie Galbraith lived nearby with his wife. He was one of my
Dad's regular drinking partners, always looking for a soft touch
and a free round. When Galbraith split with his wife, my Dad
was there with his ever-open offer of a sofa and lodgings – only
this time, I was part of the offer in Galbraith's twisted mind. I can
still see him so clearly when I close my eyes. 'You alright there,
doll?' he would slur at me when he rolled in. I hated that man
from the outset, hated him when he was still with his wife, hated
him more when he decided I was there to be pawed and abused.
He would leer over me whatever I was doing, but I thought for a
while that that was as far as it would go.

One night, he and my father staggered in. My Dad was blind
drunk as usual, and Dougie Galbraith was certainly acting that
way. For a while. I'd been home for hours, fed Karen on the
scraps I could throw together, and got her settled down for the
night after the latest chapter of the story I was making up for her
from my imagination. I was a long way from turning in for the
night. I was in sole charge of cleaning, cooking, organising,
getting myself prepared for school, making sure Karen had
clothes that were as clean and presentable as I could manage. My
Dad, oblivious to everything, stumbled through to his bed, and
collapsed, fully clothed. The stench from him wouldn't get any
better by the morning – and there was a good chance it would be
joined by some vomit and piss which would be left for me to
clean up.

Still, I checked on him. He looked like he would survive until
morning. I went back to what passed as our living room, and

Galbraith was already sitting there, legs splayed, smirk on his face, looking like he owned the place.

'That's the old man out for the count then, doll?' he asked. I couldn't even look at him. Even now, it really disgusts me to think about him. He had a gap between his front teeth, and always, always smelled of old beer and cigarettes. For some reason, he thought the height of elegance was the tightest pair of jeans he could pour himself into, and he even managed a bit of a swagger. I don't doubt for one second that Dougie Galbraith thought the single women of Edinburgh were delighted at the thought of him on the market again after his split from Jean. As my Dad lay virtually unconscious in another room, his 'mate' unzipped his welded-on jeans and took out his penis. 'Come on, doll, give's a wee bit of help here.' He held out his hand as if he was performing some great gentlemanly act. 'Sit beside me on the sofa here. We'll have a wee chat, get to know each other. You're a lovely looking wee lassie you know. Could easily have a boyfriend. Mind you, maybe you want a real man. Is that it? You holding out for Dougie?'

Galbraith's 'advances' had been pretty obvious for some time. He was a vile, lecherous man who would stare at me whatever I was doing, and always seemed to sober up remarkably quickly whenever my Dad was out of the room. Galbraith's empty compliments were a clumsy way of trying to make me feel that this was actually some sort of relationship. He would tell me I was good-looking, tell me I was worth his time – and I was so starved of affection, so ignorant of what a normal relationship was, that I actually did wonder. I walked over to the sofa where this ugly, rancid excuse for a man was asking me to masturbate him. Did I shout on my comatose Dad? Did I scream that his friend was trying to abuse his daughter? Did I even tell Galbraith where to go? No. I sat beside him, on that awful sofa, in that vile living-room and did exactly as he asked. And how did this great romantic interlude end? 'That was spot-on, doll,' he hissed through the gap in his teeth as he wiped himself off on his manky Y-fronts and shoved himself back into his skintight denims. 'Any chance of a cup of tea?'

Many people would say to me: 'Your Dad's a good man.' Many would tell me: 'Your Dad would do anything for anybody.' Many would inform me: 'Your Dad would give a man the shirt off his back.' Well, my Dad gave them a damn sight more than that. He served his daughter up on a plate too.

There were four different men who abused me over this period. I know where some of them still live. Most of them have families. They all followed the same pattern – they'd be men my Dad had met out drinking. They'd doss down on our sofa when they were down on their luck or too drunk to go home, then they'd start on me. These men were offered hospitality but took so much more. Of course, it's hard for me to talk about the specifics of these incidents because even years later the pain is still there – not just the pain of what they did to me, but also the pain which comes from knowing that, yet again, my Dad turned a blind eye. And, yet again, I thought it was all my fault. Yes, they gave me compliments and yes, I accepted their words – but how could I have been so starved of everything that I would do all of the things they demanded just for those scraps of attention? It's not just my Dad's involvement I have to pick apart – I have to go back and look at myself too, and at a child who thought she deserved such treatment time after time.

What hurts the most is that, for years, I had really believed that my Dad would save me one day. He would see it all; he would work out – at last – what was happening to me. He would get on his white steed and ride to my rescue.

Now, it hit me full in the face.

He was never going to save me.

He made things worse.

Some hero.

Chapter Seventeen

જી

HOPES AND DREAMS

IT WAS TIME FOR me to face up to facts. The only person who was going to save me was myself.

I don't get the feeling that my father wanted to be party to any of Helen's 'activities', but I can also see that he does deserve some blame, not only for what happened while she was on the scene but also for closing his eyes to the later abuses which happened. Just as she made choices and must be held accountable for her actions, my Dad also played his part. I think he was a very weak man, who for some reason, needed this awful woman so much that he not only turned a blind eye to what was going on, but also became party to some of it. He most definitely knew about the violence, and surely he must have seen that I was a bag of bones. He must have known that there were problems at school, and that I was a terrified scrap of a child. I tried to talk to him about it a few years ago when he was dying. He couldn't do it. Whatever I asked, whatever I brought up, he shook his head and looked away.

There may come a time when I want to dig still deeper but, at this stage, I don't feel a need for it because I'm so tired of trying to make sense of everything. This man should have been my hero, my protector – but he clearly wasn't.

In later years, I can accept that he had an incredibly mundane life. I know it can't have been easy having the responsibility of so many children, but my Dad just seemed to give up on everything. People thought he was so good for taking Karen on – and I do think he made the right choice there – but he also delegated to me the responsibility of looking after her, running the house and making sure he always had a settled life. While everyone in Easter Road praised Don Ford to the rooftops, they didn't seem to notice the 11-year-old mini-mum who was holding it all together.

My memories of him are very physical, very vivid. He was unable to get around easily due to the damage done to his feet after an accident he had had falling off a ladder, and I have an incredibly clear memory of him sitting on his chair with his trouser legs rolled up and his feet in a basin of hot water. His chest was in a bad way too, due primarily to his chain-smoking. No matter how little money we had, there was always enough for my Dad to get his full-strength Woodbine, Capstan or Embassy Regal. Most times, he'd buy packets of 10, but if times were really hard, one of us would be sent to the little Polish shop in Bothwell Street to buy one or two 'singles' for him. Every morning, before he could even stand up, he'd cough and splutter and spit. His day started with copious amounts of tea and a lit fag that never seemed to go out. To me, it just looked like one never-ending cigarette and cuppa. When things were really tight, he would break up all his dog-ends to make another smoke. By the time I was coming into my teens, my image of my Dad was that of an ill, coughing, smelly old man who rarely moved from his chair, which was surrounded by his copy of *The Sun*, an ashtray, a pen, fags, Bluebell matches, a beer can, a stained cup of tea, and a spare cup for him to spit in.

Dad's illness and complications got progressively worse – he ended up with curvature of the spine and severe lung problems. These conditions added to my overall feeling about him – I never respected the man, but I did pity him. By the time I left home a few years later – as soon as I could – all I could think about was my 'release'. I was delighted to move away from my past, from the Ford family, from Easter Road. When I was first engaged, one of my main thoughts was that I would soon have a new name. It's only now, writing this, that I can even face my legacy and call myself Donna Ford once more. However, that engagement also brought me to a crisis point. All major events, such as weddings, births, Christmas, make me think of family – I'm no different to anyone else in that sense – but the thoughts are bittersweet. I can't rewrite the past, irrespective of how some relatives would like me to, and neither can I ignore what I came from. But when I started to plan my wedding, I was faced with the prospect of becoming someone who was in charge of her own destiny. What would my father think of that if he knew? What would he think of me doing so well? I was feeling so positive that I really believed I was strong enough to see him again, tell him about my happiness, and maybe even invite him to the wedding.

I had already told a version of my past to my future in-laws, in which I omitted a lot of the detail and concentrated on the fact that my father and I had a 'strained' relationship. My family-to-be meant a lot to me. They were kind people and had given me the sort of family security I had only ever dreamed of as a child. When I gave them the sanitised story of Don Ford and me, they immediately suggested that we all go out for a meal together, including my father. It was agreed that we would go to the Doric Tavern in Edinburgh for an engagement celebration. I should have known better. I spent so long getting ready for that occasion. I suppose I wanted him to see how happy I was, how well I was, and to congratulate me, while at the same time recognising what he and his choices had put me through. I was proud of my fiancé, Robert, and of his parents, Bob and Flora. But my Dad was another matter. I hated every minute of that evening. From the moment I walked in, I knew it would be a disaster. I was too ashamed of him, and the pain of the past was too great to put behind me. I couldn't wait for the night to end. We barely spoke – all he cared about was the booze he was throwing down his throat, and I knew he only looked at my prospective in-laws as a free meal. There were no kind words, there was no reconciliation. I felt sick to the stomach as I left the Doric and knew it would take a lot before I would be willing to risk another encounter.

જ

Some months later I received a phone call at Bob and Flora's house. I was so happy that day. I was painting a wardrobe for Robert's nephew's birthday and he was standing behind me, leaning on my shoulder lovingly. 'Do that bit now, Auntie Donna!' he would shout as we worked on the jungle scene we had created together. All I could focus on was how right these people felt for me – they appreciated me; they encouraged my artistic leanings; I was part of a normal, loving family group. I heard the phone ring, but didn't think it would be for me until Flora called up to say my sister was on the line. I had given the number to Karen in case she ever needed to get me urgently (in the back of my mind there was always a feeling that she might need my help one day, she might need to get away quickly). 'Donna,' she said. 'It's Dad. He's had a stroke.' The words didn't come as a surprise. This man had been slowly killing himself for years – it had to catch up with him one day. 'He's in the Royal Infirmary, Donna. Are you going to see him?'

What could I say? I didn't want to visit. I didn't want to reopen old wounds. But maybe he was dying; maybe this would be my last chance. After much deliberation, I decided I did have to go. For me, not for him. I didn't want another regret to eat away at me in later years.

The day of my visit dawned. I suppose I wasn't really prepared for what I was moving towards, or what it would involve and stir up for me. The man who had put me in a children's home, taken me back again to a life of hell, married my torturer, turned a blind eye to what was done to me for years was now dying in an Edinburgh hospital and there were things I needed to know. That morning I was in a state of total confusion – I couldn't bear the thought of being associated with my father and yet, I had to get something out of this before it was too late. My life was so nice now, and I didn't want this past life with its dark memories and horrible secrets to spill over into it, tainting and tarnishing.

When I got to the Royal Infirmary, I spent a long time outside. The building itself seemed to scream depression and failure at me. Edinburgh's main hospital has now moved to another site at Little France, where it is surrounded by green fields with a view of the nearby Pentlands, but the old building was dark, dirty and ominous. The labyrinth of corridors meant that visitors had to spend a long time searching for wards and patients. As I entered the building, the stench of the place made me feel claustrophobic. Finally, I found the ward I was looking for. I walked in and saw him, stared at him as he lay there with his eyes closed. He was propped up because of his breathing difficulties, with his pyjamas on. His face was thin and drawn. He was rasping with each laboured breath. My father smelt old, even though he wasn't. There was a stink coming from him of something terrible and decaying, as if his body was finally getting rid of the years of muck he had poured into it. If he hadn't opened his eyes, I would probably have just left. He slowly opened the heavy, yellowed lids but said nothing. No words of comfort or greeting, not even my name. I went into 'coping' mode. 'Hi, Dad,' I breezed. 'How are you then?' The untruths so well known to every hospital visitor tripped off my tongue. 'You're looking well, much better than I imagined.' Lie. He looked awful. A man facing death. A man whose body was wrecked and who couldn't even bring himself to care. 'It's nice here, isn't it?' Lie. The place was full of identical old men, ignored by staff unless a 'situation' occurred in what was basically a waiting room for the morgue. 'I'll just get this all sorted then we'll have a nice chat.' Lie. We had never managed a nice chat with each other in all our lives together – it was unlikely to begin now.

I had taken the ritual bottle of squash and some flowers with me. As I busied myself arranging them and tidying up his bedside locker, I made small talk as if I had seen him only the day before. There was no one else there, no one else to take some of the burden, so when the doctor appeared at my Dad's bedside, I was the one he informed. 'Are you Mr Ford's daughter?' he asked. I had to agree – this wasn't a time to start arguing about the nausea I felt every time our familial link was made. 'Your father is very unwell,' he continued, emphasising the relationship with every phrase he uttered. 'He has suffered an aneurism – but that isn't all that's wrong. He has chronic bronchitis. He has emphysema. He is suffering from mal-nutrition. He has been told that most of this, if not all, is completely self-inflicted. Miss Ford ...' I shuddered at that name again, 'If your father does not stop smoking, we will not be able to treat him. He must make some effort on his own behalf now. He has a choice.'

Choice. That word again. I didn't know whether my father had always been very good or very bad at making choices. He could certainly ignore things that were staring him in the face – and now it was his own death he had to face up to. Maybe this would do it. Maybe this would be enough to make him take responsibility for his own actions – and if he could do that once, perhaps he could move on and tell me what I needed to know. I was vaguely aware of the doctor still talking as this all rushed through my mind. I came back to the conversation just in time to panic.

'Miss Ford? Did you hear me, Miss Ford? I was asking whether you were in a position to care for your father.'

'What? Me? No, no – I couldn't! I just couldn't,' I shouted.

He looked at me as if I was completely over-reacting. And, of course, in his eyes, with the limited information he had, I was. 'Really, Miss Ford, all I mean to impress upon you is the fact that if you could take him home and look after him, your father would stand a much better chance. It isn't a particularly difficult task, if that is your concern.'

I couldn't take this any longer. My father was lying there, oblivious to everything, while this stranger suggested I break my life again to put him first. It was all too much for me, and I became almost incomprehensible. I began to blurt out all manner of things – I screamed that there had been too much trauma in the past, that the doctor couldn't possibly understand, that there was a history I couldn't deal with. I went on and on as that poor man looked at me as if he wished he had done anything but sign up for rounds that day. He finally left, shell-shocked, and said we could talk about it another time. As he walked away, my father opened his eyes and looked at me.

'That windbag finished then?' he rasped. I nodded. 'Do us a favour then, hen – get us a fag.'

I left that day feeling absolutely wretched. I went back to visit him four or five more times but nothing was changing. He felt the world owed him something and that he need take no responsibility for his own actions whatsoever. I felt constantly guilty. I couldn't be the daughter he wanted – I couldn't erase the past – and as long as it was all there, unspoken, between us, we couldn't have anything near to a 'normal' relationship. I went through the motions each time – brought grapes, arranged flowers, made sure he had tissues, fluffed his pillows – but it was all a charade. On top of the guilt was a feeling of increasing anger towards my father. He lay there demanding so much, so much petty stuff, when he gave so little.

One day, I decided I'd had enough. I had something to say – he must have known what it would be – and I wanted some answers. Every time I saw him, the past hit me like a mallet. I was back to having nightmares, and even the loving support of my new family couldn't protect me from the memories which were rearing up again towards me. I had kept myself so busy for so long, as if filling my life could stop my mind from wandering into areas I knew could destroy me. Now I knew just how ineffectual it had all been. I went into the Royal Infirmary that day and did my usual fussing around my father's bedside. I watched him, his bones shining through his skin in his too-big hospital pyjamas. He was skinny and ancient to me. His eyes looked huge through his glasses, and he was getting closer to death every day. I knew I was going to say something, but I didn't know when, how or what it would be. As I unnecessarily rearranged the wilting flowers in the glass jar yet again, I span around to face the old man in the hospital bed.

'Why didn't you stop her, Dad?' I whispered as the tears streamed down my face. 'Why didn't you stop her?' He wasn't looking at me – had he even heard me? I couldn't stop, it all came up, no spaces, no thinking, just one, long, joined-up bundle of all the things I wanted to know. Things I had always wanted to know.

'Did you know what she did to me did you know what went on did you know about those men what they did what I suffered the assaults the rapes the abuses the torture the starving the way she treated me worse than a dog did you know Dad about the parties and what did she tell you when you came home and you must have smelled the booze and noticed the mess and known what she was doing and did you see me getting thinner Dad and did you believe her when she said I was a witch and why Dad why Dad why?'

He turned and looked at me once.

Our eyes met.

This was my father. This was the man who was responsible for me being here. He had answers. He could tell me things. He could even lie – and if it was convincing enough, I would have him back again.

He turned away without a word.

I never saw my father again and he never did give me any answers.

Chapter Eighteen

ى

FINDING DONNA

MY DAD RECOVERED SUFFICIENTLY after his stroke to be able to leave the hospital and go home. It was decided by others that he couldn't go back to his flat because he wouldn't be able to manage, so he was offered supported accommodation in Abbeyhill. Karen, who was still only in her early teens, moved with him. In the winter of 1981 he was admitted to Leith Hospital where he was treated for a chest infection, amongst other things. Just as my Dad was due to be released from that hospital, he suffered an extreme bronchial attack which resulted in his death. After much personal angst, I decided to attend his funeral. I remember very little about it. The death of my father meant so many things – I'd never get the answers to the questions that haunted me. I'd never find out what he knew or suspected. I'd never discover why he allowed it all to happen, or what hold Helen really had over him. I had been cheated again. How would I ever work out who I was, what I was, with so many pieces missing?

My feelings that day come to me only in parts. I know that I was confused. I know that I was upset – not for his passing, but for the gap I was left with. I know that I was angry – as I watched hypocrites like Dougie Galbraith stand there as if past abuses had never happened. As I stood there – a strange combination of numbness and seething emotion – I saw Dougie walk towards me. The last time I had seen this man, he had abused me. What could he possibly want? To apologise? To make some crass comment about the loss of my father?

'Donna! How are you, hen?' he questioned. 'Terrible loss. Terrible.' So that was how it was to be.

One of the many men who had wrecked my early years was standing in front of me and I was expected to collude in the game. Play along, Donna. Don't rock the boat.

He looked confused. 'Your Dad, Donna? Good man, really good man. Terrible shame.'

How dare he! He had abused my father's hospitality and then abused me. He had taken advantage of my father's gullibility, come into his home, and violated that man's child. And now, it was all water under the bridge, was it? He had such a clean conscience that he could turn up at that man's funeral? It was rubbing salt into the wound.

The platitudes continued. I heard various words about my father, his death, my loss. It meant nothing to me. I dragged my eyes up from the ground to meet those of Dougie Galbraith. I saw a flicker of recognition. Then I spat at his feet with all the hatred I could muster. He quickly turned round and walked away – and I was left wondering whether, yet again, I had missed the chance to name someone for what they truly were.

৵

Those were strange days after my father died. What was I now? What was my place? I still didn't know whether my mother was alive, and I had no contact with Helen, but half of my genetic heritage was certainly in the past. And, in some strange way, I felt freed.

I believe that I have made myself the best person I can be.

What happens to us as children obviously has an effect – we are moulded in those days – but we also have some choice about the adults we become. My mother, my father and Helen all had that choice – and, as a child, I paid the price.

After my Dad died, and to this day, I was left with so many questions for the three people who made my life what it was in those days.

I had already faced my father with the question I really needed to ask. I put it to him in his dying days. Why did he let it all happen? When he refused to answer that, when he turned away from me, I was left with another question – why couldn't he answer me? Was he too ashamed and guilty because he knew what had gone on? Or did that shame and guilt come from a too-late realisation of what an evil cow Helen was? Or was it for some other reason that I have always found too awful to comprehend or even spell out? Did he know? Did he know?

I want to think that he wished he had realised sooner, but why couldn't he even say that to me? Why did he take so much shit from her? Why didn't he stand up for himself? Why did he beat me when she told him to? I can't forgive my father for bringing Helen into my life, and neither can I forgive him for leaving me to the devices of his sick friends after she left. I want to believe that he never knew about the drunken attacks after he brought 'friends' back to the house, but he should have protected me. That's what Dads are for.

There were times when I almost touched his heart – I saw it in his eyes – but Helen was always stronger than either of us. Did he really believe her when she told him I was evil? He made excuses for her, let her get away with it, gave her permission to punish me even more, and then became actively involved by meting out beatings to me at her command.

Is that how he intended things to be? Would any father actually choose that? Opt into it? I can remember the day he took me 'home' from Barnardo's so well. I remember holding his hand so tightly and looking up at this man who would protect me. I was so proud! He was my very own Daddy.

But I was left in her hands by the man who should have been looking out for me, wasn't I? He never even bothered to tell me about my real mother – not one scrap – and that was his duty. I had a right to know. The truth means so much more to a child than speculation, but speculation was all I had.

Even at my father's funeral, I was ashamed of him. I had no love or respect for him, even at a time when we could, maybe, have made our peace with each other. I know that he is no longer here and can't answer my criticisms, but I did give him that chance and he chose not to take it. He threw that away – the same way he had thrown away my childhood. So much was now lost and, with my father's death, can never be retrieved. Little girls need a hero for a Daddy, and Don Ford was far from that.

These thoughts all race through my mind. I know that my relationship with my father (or his memory) is a complex one. My only chance of forgiving him in some way, at some point, is by looking at what I have become and what I have achieved. I am here, confident, fulfilled and happy. That is due to the people I met along my path, who in some way filled the voids my father both ignored and created. He lost out so much by not putting my needs as a child at the front of things. Because of that I pity him, I pity his wasted life. He never knew the love of his grandchildren or the satisfaction of seeing his own child happy – or the sleep which comes at night from knowing you have been a good parent.

Ultimately, I think I do forgive my father, purely because doing so makes me feel better than lifelong anger. But where he may invoke some degree of forgiveness and pity, Helen Ford can strive for neither.

ॐ

To this day, I remember how Helen could make me feel so worthless, so insignificant, in everything she did. Not just the beatings, not just the starvation or the abuse, but in every little word she made me think I was nothing. One day, barely seven years old, I was scrubbing the lobby floor in Easter Road. I got a backhander right across the face for the word I had used. The word was 'mum'. 'You will call me Mrs Ford!' she screamed. 'Not mum – I'm not your mum and never will be!' That was the voice of the woman who was supposed to be caring for me, feeding me and showing me the love of a mother. Her voice, those words, stung me as much as the beating I was in for.

Now, as the woman I have become, those words have a sweeter ring. I am overjoyed that she was not my mother and that I do not share her evil blood. I am proud of that. My only regret is that she gave birth to Karen because it is hard to believe she could have anything to do with the existence of such a lovely individual. Maybe she doesn't even remember her daughter – the dumped baby, the child abandoned at 18 months, left with a man who wasn't even her father.

Helen Ford said something in court about being a 'loving mother'. What loving mother abandons her baby? I speak from experience because it happened to me too. But leaving Karen wasn't her only crime. She stood in that court and lied, lied the same way she had done for years. Did she remember the three monkeys? See no evil, speak no evil, hear no evil. I certainly remember them well. We shook with fear, with those monkeys in our mind, telling the social workers all the lies she had battered into us. Who else did she lie to? It has to be quite a list – doctors, family, teachers, friends, neighbours. Everyone really. Ultimately, she knows what the truth is. As do I. She knows how much she hated me and wanted to destroy me, and how little she thought of my life to allow her sick, perverted friends to use me. She does know, she does, and I cling to the hope that the knowledge will finally destroy her.

࿐

I have had so much to go through when I think of my father and stepmother, and when I try to separate what they each, in their own ways, did to me from the strong woman I have become. In my quest to find the real 'me', the core of the person which hasn't been tainted by what was done, my own mother comes back to me time and time again.

I don't even know what to call her. Breda? Brenda? Mother? Mum? Who is she? Where is she? Is she still alive? I have missed her my whole life, longed for her presence my whole life. I wonder whether she has ever thought about me in all these years. Well, I've certainly thought of her. I've cried rivers of tears for the woman I never knew, for the lack of her. I wonder if she would instinctively know that – or even care. So many times in these tears, when Helen Ford beat me and her friends sexually abused me, I called for my Mummy, I cried for her to come and save me. Throughout my adolescence I needed her comfort and words. She wasn't there to see me marry, and she wasn't there to hold my babies, as the proud grandmother should have been.

I have often thought of what my Mum looked like and how much of her is in me and my children. The photographs I have aren't enough. I don't know her smell. I've no recollection of ever touching her. I expect that she found new love, made a new life, possibly had more children to replace the ones discarded in Edinburgh. But I missed out on so much by not having her in my life. As I get older, I also know that she missed out too. I think I have turned out to be a fine person. I am proud of my achievements and my three beautiful children.

I don't know if our paths will ever cross. I will never actively seek my mother, but, if she is still alive, I do want her to know that I am here if she does ever wonder about me. They say that nothing in the world can ever replace the love of a mother – I only wish I could have found out if that were true.

It still hurts that my father never spoke about Breda. When I hear people saying they are turning into their mothers, or they casually dismiss something their mums said, I feel a knife going into me. I never had that chance. I never had the opportunity to get bothered by my mother, and I still have an emptiness where those memories and feelings should be. Where Don Ford said nothing about her, Helen rarely shut up. She always spoke of her in a way that made it clear my mother was still perceived as a threat, as competition. Breda was referred to with venom. She was the one who had created me – the bastard child – with the man Helen now wanted to keep for herself. The fact that my mother was no longer around, and never would be, didn't matter to my stepmother. She didn't work with logic or good sense. I used to hang on to that story Simon had told me of Breda making daisy chains, and the gentleness he recalled. That's all I had. As a mother myself, I find it hard to believe that the woman who gave birth to us would ever have erased her three children from her memory entirely, but I have no idea of the choices she had or why she made the decisions which ended up changing my life so much. I suppose I do cling to the little things – knowing that she was Irish, always being told by Helen that I was a little Irish bitch, influenced my decision to give my youngest daughter an Irish name. The photographs I have of Breda are difficult to make out – her features are slightly blurred – but I can still see a family likeness, especially between her, myself and my eldest daughter.

It all feels like a patchwork Donna has been made. The memories, the feelings, the half-recovered ideas from records, other people, writing this book. Certainly, becoming an adult was difficult. I had to learn so many things – social skills, communication, how to trust, how to hug, how to love, how to look after myself, personal hygiene – but above all, how to become the person I wanted to be, not what I was shown as a child.

My self was non-existent. I didn't know if I had rights or that it was okay for me to have wants and needs. I was driven initially by an urgency to get away from all I'd ever known – the filth, pain, anger, mistrust and loneliness.

I've felt lonely for as long as I can remember, and have always yearned to 'belong' and to join in instead of being on the outside looking in. As time went on and I was able to get further and further away from my childhood and pick up influences on the way, I began to formulate my ideals and decide on a path to follow. I know that, as an adult, I have often trusted others too readily, but I do believe in taking people at face value and that a decision is often made instinctually.

My philosophy of life is based on fairness. You must only ever ask something of others if it is fair. I have been so very lucky that my children are all healthy, intelligent, beautiful, caring individuals. I can still recall the overwhelming feelings I experienced after the birth of my first child. I remember holding him and gazing as he fed from me. I couldn't stop thinking how lucky I was, but I also felt that this achievement was another poke in the eye to Helen. I was going to be the best mother I could be. My children were never going to know any of the pain I had known. They were individuals in their own right. One day they would be adults – and the last thing I wanted was to be responsible for rearing another messed-up individual. From the word go, they were always allowed to have an opinion, and whether we agreed or not, we discussed it and compromised where appropriate.

I have always felt that children must have boundaries for stability and security. They must be stimulated and encouraged to fulfil their potential. But, most importantly, they must be loved and know they are loved. In my view, the love given to a child must be unconditional.

I would like to think that I have got things right.

Only the legacy that is my family – the family I have made which is untainted by what was done to me – will tell whether I have succeeded.

Chapter Nineteen

૪

THE TRIAL

I WAS FIVE YEARS and one month old when I was first given to Helen Ford. I was 11 when she left the family home and I got my first taste of freedom after suffering six years of abuse and deprivation. I didn't see her again until the day I faced her in Edinburgh's High Court in October 2003.

When your life is shattered – again – is there ever any warning? When fragile little lives which have taken so much time and care to put together are casually broken, it tends to be in the middle of complete normality. People suffer such losses, such grief, every day, and they generally do so without the slightest bit of notice. In the grand scheme of things, the stuff that comes with a forewarning isn't really that important. We know when that big exam is, the driving test, a long-awaited holiday. But birth, death and the police knocking at your door tend to be a bit less predictable.

I can say it now – my name is Donna Marrianne Ford. That's the name I was born with – but only through writing this book is it a name I have chosen to repossess. For years, I have hated my surname. It reminds me – of the mother who left me, of the father who put me in a children's home, of the stepmother he brought to visit me when I was a toddler, and of the life she then made for me. I am taking that name back again, just as I am taking my life back again. I have tried to piece it all together before, but only now do I feel able to tell the whole story, and only now do I feel there is a chance I will be listened to.

~

I was living in such a gorgeous house, with such a carefully put-together life, when it happened to me in the winter of 2001. When I look back on it, I can see headings above certain days in – certain events from – my life. That one is clearly marked, 'The Day the Police Came'. On the outside, I had everything. Three happy, healthy children. A loving partner. A successful career. It had all come at a price, and it had taken so very long to get there, but I truly did feel things were going well for me.

The house we rented was in Victoria Road in North Berwick. North Berwick is a stunning coastal village about 30 minutes from the centre of Edinburgh. It is a beautiful seaside resort with a traditional harbour at its heart, which sits on the southern side of the Firth of Forth where it meets the North Sea. It is a place that just feels happy. I adored living here. Victoria Road itself was full of history – it is one of the oldest roads in the area, and archaeologists have uncovered a wealth of artefacts. This sense of the past always appealed to me – perhaps because my own past was so lacking – and I have always been drawn to tradition and folklore. Our house was near to the harbour. As an artist, I spent much of my time visiting the old part of the town, and filled many sketchbooks with images of past and present fishing life. I had come to know the old characters well, and was even planning an exhibition in which my paintings would tell of the lost trade and skills of the local area.

Things were going well for me. In addition to painting, I also took on work as a house renovator, trying to turn people's dreams into reality when they looked to add art to their homes in

whatever way. I thoroughly enjoyed this work and the satisfaction I got from bringing ideas to life. I came home from a day
spent on one of these projects to a busy house. My elder daughter
Claire and her brother Paul were there with friends, and I had
picked up their little sister, Saiorse, from her childminder. I
revelled in the buzz of a frantic house. It was something I needed.

Both Paul and Claire, at 16 and 14, were at the age when food
is the biggest concern. They scavenged around the kitchen, in and
out of every cupboard, raiding the fridge and freezer, shouting
and laughing as they all dodged each other. There was that
feeling which comes at the end of the day – when you can feel
absolutely shattered, but also totally content with your life. Even
though it was all perfectly mundane, perfectly normal, it felt so
good. My kids were settled, I was receiving critical acclaim as an
artist, and I had even met the man I would later marry.

When the doorbell rang, I didn't give it a second thought.
Even when I opened it to find two police officers standing there,
I wasn't filled with dread. That came later.

It never even occurred to me that this visit could be related to
my past. We were all safe. I hadn't done anything to be worried
about. It was probably something very straightforward – in fact,
it probably didn't even relate to me. Perhaps it was something to
do with neighbours, a break-in maybe or a car problem.

They identified themselves. I asked them in, one male, one
female officer. By now, the kids were all off doing their own
things, so we went to the kitchen. I remember the pleasantries.
Would they like tea? No, thanks. Would they like to sit down?
Yes, please. Was there anything I could get for them? Just answer
a few basic questions, thanks.

'Can we just check your identity first?' asked the woman
officer. She looked perfectly innocuous. Quite young, professional, no big sign over her head saying she was going to rip
my life apart. 'Are you Donna Marrianne Shipman? Were you
born on 5 June 1959? Is your brother Simon Robertson?' They

confirmed addresses I had previously lived at, and dates when I had been there. I answered in the affirmative to everything, and yet still nothing was falling into place.

Then the words hit me.

'Donna, we're from the Family Protection Unit of Lothian & Borders Police. We're here to tell you that Simon has made some very serious allegations. These allegations relate to how you were both treated by your stepmother, Helen Thomson Laing Ford, when you were children. We are currently investigating these claims and need to know whether there are things you would like to tell us. Is there anything you would like to add?'

Some more words started swimming about. 'You don't have to say anything just now, Donna. It's really important that you think about the implications of this. What Simon has told us is very serious indeed and you need to consider whether you want to contribute anything to any inquiry. We will have to act on any information you provide us with, so take some time before making your decision.'

I could hear them speaking, I could hear the words. I knew they were trying to be nice. This was their job and I'm sure they had both been on dozens of courses and training sessions which taught them how to deal with this type of scenario. But this was me. This was my life. And this was my past coming back to me at a time when I had finally thought it buried.

The questions kept coming. 'When did you last see or hear from your brother, Donna?' Half-brother! Half-brother, I wanted to shout – please let them get the facts right on this then everything else might be accurate too. We had the same biological mother, but different dads.

I told them that Simon had been looking for me on a number of occasions, the last one being in 1997 when I had received a few letters from the Salvation Army 'Missing Persons' Department. These letters said that Simon wanted to be in touch and that he hoped I felt the same way. I didn't. I had informed the Salvation

Army that I had no wish to contact any members of my family then or at any time, but they sent me his address 'just in case'. Why couldn't I be left alone? I had nothing in common with my half-brother other than our shared biological mother and some awful childhood memories. We were totally different people with vastly contrasting lives, and I never wanted to be reminded of what did bind us.

Now, in my home, in my kitchen, with my children playing in another room, was another assault on me and the world I had tried to make for us all. As the policewoman sat there and told me what she knew about my past, from what Simon had told her, I was too shocked to speak or move. These were shreds of my personal history which no other person had access to. I didn't want her to know. I didn't want her to bring it to my house. She told me again of the allegations Simon had made against our stepmother – but it became clear that she and her colleague didn't know the half of it. What they said, what Simon had told them, was perfectly true – but it was still sanitised; it was still so much less than what had been done to me.

She ended by saying that the police wanted to pursue a case against Helen Thomson Laing Ford. I could take as much time as I wanted to think about whether I would be involved. If I did, then I would need to give a statement or, more likely, a series of statements, to help them secure a conviction.

They stood up, gave me their contact numbers, said they'd be in touch and left. I heard the front door close as I sat there in a state of shock. I was utterly stunned. The first thing I needed to do was throw up. Once that was over, the real effect hit me. Not that I might be involved in a criminal trial against my stepmother. Not that the police had just turned my world upside down. No, the main thing that struck me was this – *they wanted to listen.*

The two people who had just left actually wanted to hear my side of the story. They were asking so much – but at least they *were* asking. And what would my story be?

Of the times she beat me from the days when I was a small child in her care?

Of the times she held a red-hot poker to my face and threatened to scar me for life?

Of the times she made me stand almost naked in a freezing cold bathroom while she tormented me?

Of the times she starved me and I stole food?

Of the times she slapped and kicked and strapped and burned me?

Of the times she held parties where her 'friends' would abuse me?

Of the times she encouraged those 'friends' to rape her step-daughter?

Of the times she sent me to neighbours to be sexually abused with her blessing?

Would they listen to all of that? Would they believe it? Would they do something about it?

To say this wasn't something I could decide overnight is an understatement. In fact, it took about six months before I gave my first police interview. My partner and friends all assured me that they would stand by me, no matter which road I decided to take. They made me feel strong and that I was in a place where I could cope with all that would emerge. But could I? Could I go back to those places? Could I go back to that terrified little girl standing cold, alone, starving, beaten and abused in a dark, empty room with absolutely nothing in her world?

I thought I could.

But where would I start?

For years I had lived my life trying to bury the past and moving on with an existence far removed from what I had as a child. When I made the decision to pursue the case against Helen and seek some form of justice, I thought I would be strong enough to do so without it affecting me negatively, but so much came to the surface as a result. The run-up to the court case was such a harrowing time for myself and my family. The pressure of the impending court case had brought forth a backlash of trauma. I was suffering from nightmares and flashbacks so real that it was as if I had been transported back to those days.

All the normal, day-to-day stuff which simply has to be done seemed insurmountable. I couldn't even go out of the house. Every morning, I woke up with such dreadful feelings of anxiety and fear that I was throwing up. And the eating problems from which I have always suffered were there with a vengeance. I had tried so hard to get over these problems by learning to cook, and enjoying food whenever possible. Now I was back to square one. The nightmares. The anxiety. The inability to keep food down. She was getting to me again. I lost so much weight that even strangers could see there was something wrong with this ghost of a woman.

I was so angry inside – but why? Nothing had really changed. I'd always had to live with what Helen had done and what she had facilitated. What was new now? I would often vent my anger on my partner and we argued constantly. We were both completely lost.

The situation got worse and worse. I lived with all of this for two years while things moved on towards the eventual court case. The material had to be prepared, statements had to be gathered, evidence had to be collated. I was living with it every moment of every day. I couldn't pack it away any longer. There were so many cancellations and false starts – usually due to Helen's defence team saying they weren't fully prepared – that I began to think it would never happen. But it did.

౩

I had to work out how I wanted to face this.

I didn't want anyone with me at the court. I wanted – and

needed – to do this on my own, and I also didn't want anyone to be tainted by it. I was going to have to speak of things I had kept inside for so long, and I had no idea how I would deal with that when the time came.

When the day arrived – Wednesday 1 October 2003 – my partner dropped me off in a side street. I was prepared for this. I was wearing old, but smart, clothes that I intended burning when the case was over. I carried a folder of my art work to remind me of the woman I was. And I had photographs of my children – just for me – to reaffirm everything that I knew was right and good in my world.

All I could think about was how I would feel when I saw her. Would I be able to cope? Would I collapse? Would I lose control? I hadn't seen Helen Ford since I was 11 years old and totally under her vindictive power. How would I react to her presence now that we were both adults? Uppermost in my mind was the conversation I had been having with my younger daughter the previous day: telling her that I was going to court and that the woman who had been so nasty to me when I was a little girl was going to be forced to say 'sorry'. If only it were that easy!

There was such a long wait before I was eventually called to the stand. I was looked after by a court social worker who tried to explain to me what would happen, but I was miles away. I was going to see her. I was going to see Helen again.

I was absolutely terrified but doing everything in my power to hide it. Everything seemed so intimidating and I knew exactly what I was so scared of – that the little Donna would come out. I was petrified that I would look at my stepmother and be taken back, that I would regress and wouldn't be able to add anything to the trial. I was trying desperately to hang on to my adult self. Every time I came into contact with someone – a court official, any other staff member – I would go out of my way to explain myself to them as an adult. I showed them my art work, I told them about my life as an artist. It was all part of me silently screaming: *I'm a different person! I'm not that scared child! I'm strong and I will do this*! This gave me so much confidence. Every time I looked at the reminders of who I was now it brought the reality of the situation home to me – I was the one in control now.

Despite what I achieved, the moment I stood in the witness box for the first time is etched on my mind for ever. I still ask myself the one question that matters most: what did I feel when I saw her again? Where can I start?

I didn't realise just how difficult it would be to face her again. My rational adult self told me that she was just a sad, tired, old woman.

Then she looked at me.

When I saw her sitting caged in behind the glass panel in the courtroom, I knew that I had won in many ways. I could stand tall and proud in the dock. I faced her not as a little girl, but as a woman who was loved, strong and respected. At that moment, I realised how pathetic Helen was. During the trial, there was a part of me that wished she would fully admit what she had done. Apologise. Look for forgiveness. She could have made an excuse – too young, too many pressures. People would probably have believed her. They may even have felt sorry for her, in the way they did when I was a child and I was always told what an angel she was, taking on Don Ford's children.

But she didn't apologise. She didn't try to excuse herself. Every time she was asked something specific about what she had done to me, she answered in monosyllables. She denied everything. There just didn't seem to be anything there. I can only think that, by now in her life, Helen Ford has told so many lies that she actually believes them herself.

The day that she was convicted was the most profound day of my life. I find it difficult even now to find words to express how I felt. I sat almost directly behind her, staring at her profile as she fidgeted with her hair and squirmed in her seat. It was surreal.

The courtroom was packed – and I wondered why. What did people hope to hear and see? What would be a 'good day' for them? The trial had been held in a closed court until the day of the verdict, but now it was full to bursting point.

I was still so nervous and worried – mostly because I thought no one would believe me, as I remembered her saying all those years ago. I couldn't conceive for one minute that Helen Ford would be found guilty. When the word was finally said, my reaction was audible. I just couldn't help the long, deep sigh and the cry of 'Yes!' that came from me. I was shaking, smiling and crying all at the same time.

Now I could look at her.

And she was a pathetic sight.

This was my vindication – what goes around, comes around.

She was guilty – and, as if that wasn't enough, Lord Hardy, who presided over the case, made it clear that he wished he could have done more. Helen Ford was sentenced to two years' imprisonment on charges of sexual procurement. The judge said, directly to me: 'I wish it could have been more.' That meant so much – he believed me and so did others. Finally.

ॐ

Once the trial was over and the verdict reached, the fear passed. Now I don't pity her or hate her – I don't really feel anything for her at all. I can't forgive her – not because I don't have forgiveness in me, but because her crimes are actually unforgivable. She will have to seek her own retribution, if she can. I can't go down the road of feeling bitter because that would affect me, not her. She will already have made her own assumptions about how I feel, but she can't really know what is in my heart. I don't want my feelings for her to take anything away from me or the strength I have found. I understand the damage that was done to me and know that it will come up at times, but I need to keep it in one place. I know that there are others who can't do that and who need revenge.

When I read the newspaper reports of the trial, I am amazed that my life, all those years, can be summarised in so few words. One is entitled: '*Woman tells court of abuse at age five.*' In only 145 words, it attempts to relay the horrors of my life. I am interested in what they perceive to be the 'highlights': 'A little girl was beaten, starved and held prisoner in a darkened room to be sexually abused ... the alleged victim was often so hungry that she ate bread left out for the birds ... she also described being beaten black and blue with a belt and said men visited her room during drink parties ... the woman said she was once made to eat from a dog bowl and was held up to a mirror and told she was an ugly witch.' That's me – I'm that little girl, and that is the sum total of what was done to me. It seems so slender, so *quick* when it's written down that way.

No matter what I think of the past and of the trial, it's time to move on. I'm left with so many questions from my childhood, and some new ones too. Now that Helen has spent time in jail, I wonder whether she has been punished. Was she fed, or starved? Was she beaten? Humiliated? Did monsters come into her bed in her tiny room and abuse her in the dark? Was she treated worse than a dog?

I don't even know what I honestly hope the answers to those questions are.

Chapter Twenty

ॐ

WHERE ENDINGS LIE ...

LIKE EVERYONE, I HAVE my bad days. Sometimes I don't know why; sometimes I don't even know what I'm feeling. At other times, I know exactly what's going on, what the questions are, where I feel the gaps still exist.

There is so much of my childhood that I have no words to describe, and there are other parts which I can only verbalise and analyse as an adult. That little girl who was me just couldn't work out what was happening in the way an adult would. I know the words now. I know the consequences. I can apply morality and judgement and principles to all of this. And that is what hurts and angers me so much.

As a grown-up, I can't make sense of how such damage can be voluntarily inflicted on a child. How can an adult choose to do these things? What makes a person decide that she will bring men to the family home to abuse her stepdaughter? What makes a woman send that child to strange men for her starved body to be attacked? What makes those men – fathers, brothers, grandfathers – believe it is permissible, justifiable, to rape a child? How can these perfectly ordinary citizens go about their business on a day-to-day basis, knowing what they have done and what they continue to want to do? How do abusers actually deal with the fact that their own needs, their own so-called desires, mean that children will be living their own personal hells?

It is the adult who knows what they are doing, who knows the words and the language for what is going on. I firmly believe that nothing an adult goes through as a child excuses them continuing the cycle of abuse which so many choose. And it is a choice, let's make that quite clear. If those who believe the cycle cannot be broken are right, what does that say about me? All I can say in my defence is that I know the person I am. I haven't been broken. I haven't been changed into some monster who cannot escape her past. If I was nothing more than a victim of what went before, my own children – my flesh and blood – would now be living the nightmare I endured. At no point was that ever an option. I have to say to those who think we victims cannot escape, to those who think that continuing abuse can be explained away by past horrors, that at no point did I have to fight any desire to turn into an abuser.

When I looked at my babies, when I raised my children, all I felt was love and a desperate need to protect them. They are not wrapped in cotton wool, and never have been. For me, the measurement of my success as a mother has been that my children are that word we are all scared of using these days – they are 'normal'. They laugh, they cry, they play, they have dreams. They have good times and bad times, but there is nothing that would ever stop me from doing absolutely everything in my power to give them a safe haven. And I do have that power. I know that now. It has taken me a while to get there, and my children have helped me on the journey, but I have never been a sacrificial lamb to my own history. Those who claim that all 'survivors' spend their time either fighting, or succumbing to, their pasts insult all of us who know differently.

My past won't go away. I am no different to anyone else in the sense that it made me who I am – the irony being that what I endured was so awful that it took parts of me away at the same time as it built me up. One of the reasons I needed to write this book was to make sense of that strange combination. How could something so bad not have broken me entirely?

Anyone who has experienced abuse as a child will process it in their own way – I never wanted this to be a self-help manual for survivors. Within my own family, different people have different stories to tell and they must find their own way, their own peace. But I know that the way forward for me was to tell my story – because, finally, I know that it is *mine*. What I went through was caused by others, by their choices, by their depravities, but the eventual culmination of it all is *me*. I have needed to possess that in order to reach any sort of closure with my past, and I know that now is the time to do it.

This is the right thing for me. I knew absolutely that I would never get the inner peace I have sought for so long unless I told my story – only the time and the way of doing it had to be right. That ring on the doorbell on that fateful day when my past truly came back to me, it was an opportunity – not one I willingly went after at the time, but one I have chosen to follow through. The trial afforded me the opportunity to say certain things, but any court process has its own format which will allow victims only a certain degree of voice. However, I am grateful both for the opportunity to say what I did at that time and in the period leading up to the trial, even if it did only scratch the surface. Going beyond that surface has opened up so much more, so many wounds, so many bad memories. At this point, I truly believe that the more we speak about these things – the more we open up to the realities of some children's lives – the more we will move towards attitudinal change.

What happened to me was taboo. It went on behind the closed doors of a private home, but the collusion was deeper. I am still incredulous that so many people, so many authorities, did nothing, did not see, did not hear. Although many adults were involved in my life, I know of no one who ever did anything about my plight. There were so many who could have acted – Barnardo's, social workers, teachers, neighbours – and who could have changed this story, but who made their own choices. The choice to do nothing.

No child should go through what I did. If, by telling my story, I can make one person think about what they can do to help a child, I have achieved something. When I was a child, there came a point when it was beyond my wildest dreams that anyone would ever pay heed to me, let alone listen to my story. Finally, someone did. But it was too little, too late.

I have spent my adult life trying to take myself away from my own childhood. Now, in my mid-40s, I desperately want to be rid of the heavy heart, anxieties and insecurities which I inherited from the abuse doled out to me by my stepmother. I've spent most of my adult life with my past buried as deep as I could possibly shove it. Now, as an adult, I believe in fairness and in balance. It's time to write my own ending, even if it has taken me this long to find any sort of peace. The little girl without the voice has finally found that she can shout.

Rearing my children to become happy, centred individuals has been the main focus of much of my adult life, coupled with the ongoing nurturing of my career as an artist. Writing this book meant exposing my soul and bringing into the light the darkness of the abuse I suffered. I had to think long and hard about doing that. I am leaving a legacy here – and such a thing cannot be undertaken lightly. My children can now read my story without distortion, but what will it do to them and to my relationship with them? How much do any of our children truly know of us? We are their mothers and fathers; we should be their rocks and their safety nets. My children have had those things, but now their mother has told her story, I have had to consider how that will impact on them. Will they want to know all of my story? Will it alter how they view me? Will it change how they act as adults and future parents?

It was not easy for me to assent to an investigation into my childhood which would lead to the prosecution of my stepmother. However, I thought that if I could achieve some form of catharsis and an understanding of why, despite being relatively happy, I suffered from inexplicable guilt, fear and anxiety, then the whole process would be worth it. The reality, churning up the past, has been difficult to the point of unbearable at times. The pain has resonated through my life, stopping me in my tracks. At times I have been unable to function. For two years I was sick every morning and crippled with anxiety. I couldn't sleep for fear of nightmares. My relationship with my new husband was tested to the limit, and I had to explain as well as I could to my children what had gone on.

So why did I do it? As I have said before, it was necessary for me to tell my story, if only for the purpose of giving a voice to the child I was. A voice that should have been heard all those years ago. I know my story is shocking but for me it was reality – a reality I lived through with no choice. There have been a number of books in recent years which have told of the personal experiences of others who were abused in some way; in many ways that is heartening. However, if all that we have managed to do is to develop a new form of 'entertainment', it has all been for nothing.

I don't know if this book will touch anyone else in any way but it is my hope that there may be some lessons to be learned. I not only survived heinous abuse but went on to become a success in my own right. I pride myself on my parenting skills and rejoice in my talent. I am blessed to have the love and support of some very fine and respected people, without whose caring I could not have found the courage to travel this journey.

I believe if we have a story to tell then it should be told. Although mine is not a pleasant one, I hope it will bring encouragement to others. I have achieved my parenting goals, to rear my children to be loved, respected, valued and individual without fear, remorse or guilt. I have successfully nurtured my artistic talent enough to enable me to enjoy a career from something I love. I also have valued, caring friendships based on love, trust and respect. These are my successes. They show my stepmother that she did not break me. They are my *raison d'être*.

My story should also bring a warning of how we must all, as adults, be vigilant. Even if that means risking retribution by sticking our necks out to protect any child whose welfare we are in any way concerned about, we must do it.

Most importantly, telling this story allows me to close those chapters in my life. I don't want to live in the shadow of these memories for a moment longer. I want, need and deserve the opportunity to find the inner peace I have always known could be mine.

After reading this, you may be shocked at the behaviour and actions of this woman, this Helen Ford, and how others also took advantage of such an appalling situation. As a mother I will never, ever understand her actions – but the important thing is that I no longer fear her. And I now know that I can live with the understanding that I was not to blame for her actions.

For me, this is not just about what was done to that child all those years ago, but the long-term effects of growing up with that history. It is also about you, the reader. You chose to pick up this book and read it to this point, and I am curious to know what you're thinking. Has it been a 'good read'? Did you 'enjoy' it? Perhaps you counted your blessings at various points, or perhaps it reminded you of something which you suffered. Maybe you are even an abuser yourself – there is a possibility that you bought this book because you hoped to find pleasure in the tale of a wrecked young life. You may have been looking for a sexual thrill or for some handy hints about how to keep your own perversions hidden or make them more successful. There is also a chance that you don't believe a word of what I say. You may have checked the Internet to see whether Helen Ford really was convicted, whether she even existed, and seeing that the case was real, you may still want to deny it all.

I think I can understand all of those reactions because I have considered many of the responses to this story while revisiting it. No matter which camp you fall into, I would like you to remember one thing.

I had to learn how to hug.

I didn't know how.

You don't have to believe every word that has been written here – I know it's all true, but you will have your own reason behind your interpretation of it. But please think about what I have just said. I didn't know how to hug someone. I didn't know how to have that natural, innocent, basic contact. Is that a remnant of a normal childhood? Is that a consequence of a natural upbringing?

For those who love me, I wish to convey not only my story but the complexity of being me. I want them all to know how vital their role has been in my development as an adult through the love and support they have offered. I want to appeal to everyone else that they always think of the child at the centre of any story. Children have a right to be loved, valued, respected, cared for, heard, nurtured and fed.

There may be people who feel uncomfortable at some of the content of this book, for reasons only they will know. But whoever you are, I ask that you consider your role in the life of any child with whom you come into contact. It is terrifying to think how much power we have over children and how easy it can be to abuse that power. The strongest in any society are the ones who put the rights of children first. The weakest, the most pathetic, the most worthy of condemnation, are those who decide that their needs take precedence over those rights.

If you are strong enough to be one of those people who put children first, through any contact you may have with them, then you have made a contribution. I don't say that with lightness, because I know what it is to desperately hope that someone will change things. Even now, I can't express what it would have meant to me if someone, some adult, had decided that enough was enough. The scraps of kindness I did experience showed me that goodness did exist – I just couldn't understand how so little of it ever came my way.

Things are changing for me, but as you have been reading this, a child will be living a nightmare. They will be being starved or raped or beaten or humiliated or any one of the thousand things that good people don't want to think or do anything about. They could be your son or daughter, another family member, a neighbour, a child you teach, a child you see each morning on your way to work, a child that bothers you by their behaviour or attitude. Those children are all around us, but we don't really see or hear them. It is your choice whether you, as an individual, allow that to continue.

My story ends here for now – my life does not.

Becoming the woman I am from the stepchild I was has been a long, involved process with no shortcuts. But I'm getting there. I'm getting there.

Thank you for listening.

At last.

Also available from Vermilion

LIVING ON THE SEABED

Lindsay Nicholson

'The morning after John's death, I remember feeling absolutely enraged that the world had kept turning and the sun had come up as if nothing had happened.'

Lindsay Nicholson and her husband, the *Observer* journalist John Merritt, were regarded as a golden couple. But their world was turned upside down when John contracted leukaemia. His death at the age of 35 left Nicholson bereft with grief, now the single parent of two beautiful daughters. Then, in a tragic twist of fate, her elder daughter Ellie also contracted the same disease, dying shortly after. Nicholson found that nothing could prepare her for the emotions she was feeling.

In this courageous and heart-rending memoir, Lindsay Nicholson reflects on her grieving process and the battle she faced to survive it. Her resilience and spirited determination are an inspiration to us all.

Also available from Vermilion

LOVE CHILD

Sue Elliott

Adoption is one of the great, untold stories of our recent past. It is a truly epic tale of loss, guilt, identity, family feuds, reunion and redemption.

In this moving memoir, Sue Elliott tells her own story of growing up as an adopted child. She details her emotional search for, and meeting with, her birth mother, Marjorie, the heartbreaking tale of how Marjorie came to give her up for adoption in the 1950s, and the shock of finding that she, Sue, wasn't the only child given away by Marjorie. Over the course of her emotional journey Elliott draws on a range of intimate personal experiences and exposes the human consequences of adoption.

Also available from Vermilion

IT'S NOT LIKE THAT, ACTUALLY

Kate Carr

It is impossible to go back to the old life after a cancer diagnosis; the reality of surviving is complex. Kate Carr was diagnosed with breast cancer at the age of 39 and underwent extensive harrowing treatment. In 2002 she was told that she'd reached a significant milestone – the five-year mark. Reaching this point without the cancer returning is a strong indication that the treatent has been successful. The sad truth, however, is that, like all cancer sufferers who have reached this stage, she had to live every day with the knowledge that it can come back at any time.

It's Not Like That, Actually charts Kate's diagnosis and treatment, while explaining in beautifully written detail the ups and downs – the reality – of moving on from there and dealing with the emotional burden that friends and family find difficult to understand.

ALSO AVAILABLE FROM VERMILION